Museum Librarianship
SECOND EDITION

Museum Librarianship

SECOND EDITION

Esther Green Bierbaum

McFarland & Company, Inc., Publishers
Jefferson, North Carolina, and London

Frontispiece: Research Library at The Mariners' Museum, Newport News, Virginia (photograph courtesy of the museum).

Library of Congress Cataloguing-in-Publication Data

Bierbaum, Esther Green.
  Museum librarianship [second edition] / Esther Green
Bierbaum.
      p.   cm.
  Includes bibliographical references and index.
  ISBN 0-7864-0867-7 (softcover : 60# alkaline paper) ∞
    1. Museum libraries—Administration.   2. Museums—
Information services—Management.   I. Title.
  Z675.M94B53   2000
  027.6'8—dc21   00-60578

British Library cataloguing data are available

Cover image ©2000 Eyewire

Manufactured in the United States of America

*McFarland & Company, Inc., Publishers
  Box 611, Jefferson, North Carolina 28640
  www.mcfarlandpub.com*

To Martha and Wayne, for patience and forbearance
beyond filial duty
And to the memory of Lester E. Asheim,
scholar, mentor, and friend

Acknowledgments

One never works alone; my colleagues in museums and libraries have been a deep well from which I have drawn. Members of the Museums, Arts and Humanities Division of the Special Libraries Association have offered encouragement and moral support, along with the intellectual and informational kind. And again I have found that my students, who patiently endured those war stories (and who now have their own to relate), taught me more than they learned from me about questioning minds and questing spirits.

I want especially to thank Corey Williams, then a graduate assistant in the School of Library and Information Science at the University of Iowa, for her dedicated ingenuity in tracking down obscure references, as well as the SLIS faculty, who welcomed me with renewed friendships, office space, copier, and bottomless coffee during my recurrent bouts of resident research.

As a sign of the times in which we live and work: I need to thank the many colleagues whom I have never seen—indeed, who are known to me mainly by an email address—but who took time in a busy day to find things, answer queries, and generally do what librarians have been doing since Callimachus opened shop in Alexandria. Where error has been made in fact or interpretation, it is, of course, my error and my lack of perception.

And to family and friends who endured much: It's back to normal, whatever normal was.

Contents

Acknowledgments   vii

Preface   1

1. Beginnings
Libraries, Museums, and Archives   5

2. On the Shelves
Developing the Library Collection   19

3. Technical Services
Organizing the Collection   39

4. Nuts and Bolts
Space, Furnishings, Equipment, and Security   59

5. Administration
People, Planning, Budgets, and Marketing   73

6. Information Services
Some Basics   95

7. Being Special
Extended Information Services   115

8. Bits & Bytes
Technology in the Library   129

9. Partnership
Libraries and Museums   149

Appendix A
Museum, Library, Archives: Official Definitions   163

Appendix B
Hypothetical Collection Development Policy   165

Appendix C
A Step-by-Step Tutorial: Constructing Bibliographic Records
According to ISBD/AACR2R Standards   169

Appendix D
Sources of Catalog Cards and Cataloging Copy   173

Appendix E
Standard Filing Rules   179

Appendix F
Hypothetical Museum Library Budgets   181

Appendix G
Related Associations and Organizations   183

Index   185

Preface

This second edition of *Museum Librarianship* has the same purpose as the first: to serve as a guide to libraries and their information services in the special environments called *museums*. *Museums* is a broad term that includes such varied repositories as science and nature centers, historical societies, aquariums and zoos, and specialized collections of items ranging from mollusks to medical instruments.

I also cheerfully admit to a previous bias: the viewpoint that museum libraries are an integral entity within museums, supporting and serving the parent organization according to the policies and standards agreed upon by both library and museum administrations. Consequently, this book emphasizes functions and services more than place—but not more than people.

And so this book is about the library *in* the museum and how it supports what goes on in the museum: acquiring and studying objects, preparing exhibits, developing programs, and conducting research. The book is not about the museum's objects; instead it describes ways to find, acquire, organize, and interpret the documentary records that illuminate the objects. Nor does the book deal with mounting exhibits or measuring audience response, but rather with enhancing the scholarship of the curators, the creativity of the exhibitors, and the skill of the educators.

The book is only indirectly about the museum profession, although it discusses strengthening the professional stance of administrators and staff. It does not neglect the library's interest in visitors and members, but emphasizes the library's role in helping the museum enhance the pleasure and knowledge gained by its visitors. But in advocating libraries, it does not shy away from suggesting ways of enhancing the libraries' status within their parent organizations.

Most importantly, this book is not about the library as a storage area for books and magazines, but as a resource for *information services*—a group of functions supporting the museum, its agenda, and its activities. Consequently, I have made some assumptions:

- **Size** is not so important, after all.

  The first edition of this guide to library and information services was directed primarily to libraries in museums self-defined as "small," with an implicit assumption that "large" museums would have the resources either to have already established a library or to secure the services of a professional librarian to carry out that goal. Not so, complained readers; large museums were in need of guidance, sometimes in establishing a library, but more often in revitalizing a dormant collection into an integral part of the museum's mission and service.

  Consequently, the focus of this edition has shifted slightly from starting up a library to emphasizing the goals of library and information services in a museum and the processes through which such services can be achieved. Large museum or small, the steps undertaken are very much the same.[1]

- **Subject matter** matters.

  What is said about the subject matter of the museum—and hence of its library—must be applied to the local museum and its library. Parent museums discussed in this book tend to house objects and information from the fields of history, natural history, science, and technology more often than from the fine arts. This emphasis arises, in part, from the author's background, but it also speaks to the prevailing needs of museum librarians: a much larger body of literature is already available for fine arts museums and their libraries. Moreover, the scholarship in fine arts has a stronger print relationship and library tradition and a somewhat different set of information needs and services.[2] Additionally, the libraries themselves have a specific library organization, the Art Libraries Society/North America (ARLIS/NA). This book, then, is of use to all museum librarians, but it will be more germane to some than to others.

- **People** count.

  This book is addressed to museum staff engaged in starting a library, revitalizing a dormant information resource, or evaluating library and information services. Thus we assume that readers will be advocates for the library—individuals in the museum who are endowed with zeal and who want to create information services, reactivate a dormant library, or extend the role and scope of an active library.

I have tried to bear in mind that starting a library or revitalizing a slumbering service is a project often undertaken in the absence of, or with only occasional help from, a professional librarian. While the author regrets that some museum libraries are not served by an information professional, the library and museum literature indicates that there is little likelihood of a change in the situation. This book cannot—and should not—take the place of an information professional if such a person's services are available even on a part-time and voluntary basis. In such a case the book can be used to supplement professional advice.

The book should also be useful to an information professional who has had no work experience in museums, and as a resource for the special library student investigating the museum library field. Thus the book looks at *why to* as well as *how to*, explaining practice as well as describing it. Experienced museum librarians, though much of the book will tread ground familiar to them, may wish to consider the issues raised in chapter 9 in respect to their local institutions.

Because it is inevitable that most museum libraries will find that information technology is only a modem, a cable connection, or a microwave dish away, attention is paid to preparing today's paper environment for tomorrow's online resource. In this regard, I have tried to bring this edition up to date in terminology and technology—while knowing at the same time that nothing is truly up to the minute in a nanosecond world. The appendices, for example, include lists, how-tos, and Web sites that will be useful to any stage of the library enterprise. I have also included some of the most recent studies and thinking about museums and libraries.

Rather than relegate bibliographical resources to the back of the book in a massive chunk of pages, I have listed relevant books, articles, and online sources at the end of each chapter. Not all of these resources are mentioned in text or endnotes (some are truly "Further Reading"), while a few items appear in the reading suggestions for more than one chapter.

I have included Internet and other electronic resources on the premise that, even though the museum or the museum library may not have online connections, most readers will have some means of access to that cybermass, either at home or through their public library. A *caveat*: electronic addresses are ephemeral; even the Library of Congress relocates its files from time to time.

There is such a wide variance among museums—and thus among museum libraries—that often general principles are stated, while the specifics, such as the core titles in a reference collection, are left to the judgment of the librarian.

Also, because archives and archives management is a specialized field, this book considers archives in relation to museums and libraries, offering suggestions for archives management as it falls under the purview of the library.

There are other changes: collection development and management now has a chapter separate from technical services and collection organization. The discussion of furnishings and equipment considers accommodations for computers and other technologies. Chapter 5, "Administration," now expands the discussion of staff to include performance evaluation and professional development, looks at fees and use-charges as budget issues, and treats library marketing as a staff and administrative role. The OPAC (online catalog) and the Internet have been added to chapter 8, "Technology," which still includes the "low-tech" information pertaining to the paper environment.

The final chapter examines the library and museum partnership, both actual and potential. It considers the nature of data, information, and knowledge— matters mutual to libraries and museums—and the beckoning future of their roles in exchanging data, creating information partnerships, and helping to increase the depth and breadth of knowledge in a world of the five-second sound bite. I believe it is in this partnership of libraries and museums that the future lies for both.

My immediate goal for this book is, then, to offer guidance in planning and providing information services in a museum. And my underlying, not-so-hidden agenda is to help enhance and enrich the encounter of the museum-goer with enduring objects, in a time when we all seem to be assailed by random noise and flickering images.

Notes

1. However, the library administration literature seems biased toward "larger," so that in regards to their staffing, resources, and procedures, active libraries in larger institutions are more like the libraries about which textbooks have been written, while small libraries—and small museums and their libraries—are left pretty much to fend for themselves.

2. Long ago, A. J. Meadows noted in *Communication in Science* (London: Butterworth's, 1974) that scientists tend to use the library's collections as documentary records of findings, while depending upon colleagues and information sources *other than* the library for current research. Subsequent investigations have supported his thesis; indeed, the development of email and other computer-based communication systems has reinforced this tendency. Such a tradition within the scientific disciplines apparently influences the level of library support in science museums, while on the other hand, art research depends and builds upon printed resources such as monographs and treatises, journals, exhibition catalogs, and graphic reproductions.

Chapter 1

Beginnings: Libraries, Museums, and Archives

This book is about beginnings and re-beginnings: establishing a library in a museum or revitalizing one that is languishing there, and then administering it effectively thereafter.

Before those undertakings, however, we need to come to an understanding of what we are talking about and an agreement on the nature of libraries and their role in particular settings. This chapter will survey ground common to all libraries and will relate concepts in organizational studies and management to our library situations.

Libraries, Museums, and Archives

Libraries, museums, and archives—or, rather, their collections—are the community's memory. But they do more than collect: they are stewards of our culture and history, of the world and our place in it; they help us understand what otherwise would remain a mystery. They capture for us things we could never know, allow us to experience what we otherwise can only dream. Unlike the other message-bearers clamoring daily for our attention, they give us room to inform ourselves and to engage in dialogue.

The definitions of these three institutions (see Appendix A) make it clear that they share many characteristics: professional oversight, collecting and organizing activities, and providing access to the collections or the information in them. Their common purpose is to gather, describe, organize, and study the records and artifacts of human thought, feeling, and activity. In short, they communicate with us about something deemed important. Carr calls them "institutions for the mindful life."[1] They also are established, permanent organizations, enjoying public recognition.

There are, of course, differences. Peter Homulos places the institutions on a continuum, with libraries at one end, museums at the other, and archives in the middle according to such considerations as collections, documentation, automation, and interaction with the public.[2] Essentially, libraries tend to collect printed materials; archives, to gather manuscripts and documents; museums, to bring together objects and icons.

In their earliest history, however, little distinction was made among the three institutions. Various kinds of materials, for instance, were collected and studied side by side in the great museum-library of Alexandria.

Such multi-faceted collections are still found to some degree. Even though the British Museum has now, under reorganization, given way in the print arena to the British Library, the museum remains a venerable model of museum-archives-library, wired-up though it may now be.[3] We also have in the United States the phenomenon of *presidential libraries*, which are primarily archival, with museum and library elements mixed in.

Indeed, there are probably few pure instances of these organizations: archives collect the papers of important persons but may also include the subjects' eyeglasses and fountain pens; museums preserve documents relevant to the collection or to objects in it; and libraries, as the scope of media expands, offer carriers of information in print, nonprint and three-dimensional formats. Moreover, all three now share a new enterprise as they engage in tackling the globally oriented resources of the Internet and World Wide Web.

Libraries in Museums

Why a library?

The case for museum support of the museum library is not clear in the literature. For example, *Museums for a New Century*, the visionary report issued by the American Association of Museums (AAM), was silent on the subject of museum libraries.[4] And the silence has yet to be broken.[5] Even in such practical situations as museum accreditation, the library is not crucial; while it is included in the AAM accreditation standards, there has been little correlation between accreditation of the museum and the museum's library services.[6]

The image of the library as mere book storage area or as the place one goes (with realistic lack of expectations) to answer a question by consulting bedraggled, irrelevant, or outdated materials has lingered on. Probably the most difficult task in establishing or reactivating library and information services in a museum is overcoming this threadbare definition of libraries. The library model we will describe in this book is no storage area but an active—even interactive—organization, with more emphasis on what goes on in the place than on the place itself.

There are lots of not-so-good reasons for a museum library. Some of the more common are because XYZ Museum has one; because somebody on the board, staff, or guild thinks the museum should have one; because it will give volunteers something to do; because it will provide a nice meeting place; because a professional association asks on its directory information data sheet whether the museum has a library.

Better answers to Why a library? are based on what a library can do for the museum when it provides timely, accurate, useful information services and resources. Here, then, are four specific benefits for the museum thus served:

- Enhancement of museum programs and services
- Support for museum scholarship and interpretation
- Saving of staff time (which translates into saving of museum money)
- Cultivation of goodwill and positive public relations

Obviously, the answer to *why* depends a great deal upon the library model—that is, on the answer to the next question, What is a library?

What Is a Library?

Incipient libraries lurk in most museums. Museum staff tend to look at a shelf of books and magazines stashed somewhere and then self-report the presence of a "library" in national directories. Indeed, surveys I conducted in 1994 and again in 1999 indicate that about a fourth of the museums are reporting such stashes.[7] But a stash does not a library make. In his brief guide for nonlibrarians, John Moorman defines a library as

> a system for collecting and storing materials for the library users, and then for organizing and circulating these materials so that they can be *retrieved* when needed.[8]

Thus, even though the museum's collection of materials (book and nonbook, print and nonprint) may be gathered together, and even organized, the museum does not have a library until that collection is located in a place dedicated to library and information services and overseen by someone charged with responsibility for two things: first, planning for daily functions and activities, including a program of services based on the needs of museum staff and library users; and second, thinking about and planning for the future.

And so, even when there is a place called "the library," and even if it is artfully arranged in a room with tables and chairs and someone sitting at a desk, until information is sought and exchanged and information needs anticipated and fulfilled, the museum is giving space to passive book storage rather than to active library and information services.

The foregoing cautionary notes and the American Library Association definition in Appendix A suggest the elements of a library considered in this book. A library, as we shall define it, has

- *someone in charge*, someone alert to users' needs;
- an *organized, accessible collection* of print and nonprint materials and resources, suitable to the museum, together with provision for access to resources not held in the library;
- a *place* dedicated to housing library materials and the services associated with them;
- *information services* to the museum community, based on the collection, the community's needs, the library's resources, and the resources available to the library.

The library in the museum, then, is an integral part of the museum, not an out-of-the-way room or set of shelves in the staff lounge (although the latter situation is much to be preferred to the former), and certainly not a frill to be tacked on when the museum is big enough and rich enough.

The library supports the museum at all points and in all phases of the museum's mission. The library will serve the information needs of administrators and staff through its own resources or through access to other resources; it may preserve graphic materials for the exhibit staff or show where they can be obtained; it may preserve the archives of the museum or provide the archivist with necessary information about the institution and its history; and, when the time comes, it will enlarge the museum experience for the members—and the public—by providing further information and resources about the collections.

Libraries in museums are *special libraries*, a category that includes any library which is neither a public, academic, nor school library. Special libraries represent a vast array of settings, subject matters, collections, and purposes—from the library serving an international corporation to the collection supporting the staff in a small social service agency. The scene is complicated by the fact that medical and law libraries are often placed in other categories, while the librarians in special collections and subject areas in academic and public libraries many times regard themselves as special librarians.

The term "special library" is itself rather unsatisfactory; in fact, John Cotton Dana, who coined it for the first meeting of special librarians in 1909, regarded it as a temporary catch-all until someone came up with something better. "Special library" stuck, however, and was institutionalized in the organization's name, the Special Libraries Association (SLA).[9]

The guiding principle of special librarianship, that *the special library exists to support the parent organization and to make its work more effective*, suggests a supportive, utilitarian function and clearly disassociates the special library from the stereotype of the library as musty heaps of deadly tomes, with cowed readers being shushed into silence amid a pervasive air of ineffective gentility. It is an active source of information and resources, not a warehouse; it supplies information and resources in all forms, not just from books.

Where a Library?

The *where* of services and resources is often a question that precedes *what* or even *why*. The idea of *place* is inherent in the notion of *library*, probably once again because of the lingering storage concept.

In special libraries, particularly those using more electronic resources than print materials in serving corporations or technical centers, the matter of place is less important than the provision of services. In such information centers, the person with the need for data or information probably does not venture near the place from which he or she receives the response.

Organizations such as museums are, however, less willing to dismiss the concept of libraries as place; the physical setting is an important consideration. The place need be neither elaborate nor large, but it should be dedicated to library functions and services and certainly should not be shared with other museum functions during the hours of active library service. Moreover, any after-hours activities should be appropriate to the setting—committee meetings, for example, but not basket-weaving workshops.

How a Library?

When the *why* and *where* hurdles are negotiated, there is the *how*. *How* is the theme of this book. Starting a museum library may mean starting from scratch, but it is more often a matter of developing and enhancing the administration of some sort of collection already there, and services that probably are not. In general there are three starting levels: no library; some books and journals in a place, but not much else; an on-going operation needing to enlarge or enhance collections and services. For the most part, this book will outline and describe procedures for the first and second starting points, keeping in mind those lurking libraries. Participants at the third level, revitalizing and enhancing library services, will recognize the place where they come aboard.

An indispensable element in starting a library is funding. The library must compete for resources within the museum and justify its claim to support. Effective collections and productive information services help refute the belief that the library is a frill. But then, because collections and services require funding to be effective and productive, we are faced with something of a catch-22. For this reason, visionary, persevering advocates are essential even *before* beginning the library.

Ideally, the library should have its own budget, established from the start.[10] The participants in the library adventure, knowing their own museum best, can determine the nature and mechanism of funding. Often a start-up grant is made, either internally or from external funding agencies.[11] Funding levels should also be projected for the years after the grant money expires.

Successful museum libraries have used other strategies, though. Fund-raisers such as book sales, paid admissions to book talks and teas, endowments and memorials—all have been successful somewhere. Krystyna Wasserman, for example, has outlined the role of gifts and contributions to the library in the National Museum of Women in the Arts.[12]

The matter of museum budget—and, in fact, the viability of the whole project—depends upon the goodwill and willingness of the museum's administrators. As Odile Tarrête states succinctly,

> Let one thing be perfectly clear: the museum library cannot fully play
> its role unless it is recognized and supported by the museum's admin-
> istration.[13]

Presenting the case for beginning or revitalizing the library to the museum's board and administrators is a challenge to be met head-on and early on. It will require research and future-gazing, with library advocates answering the *why* by looking at other libraries in similar museums; conducting an information audit within the museum;[14] and gathering data from the visits and surveys, and from the literature.[15] Visits and similar research can become the basis for projections of use and cost. The *where* is often involved as well. Whenever possible, other museum staff should be involved in the research and planning. Their support is almost as crucial as that of the board and administrators.

And finally, but not least in the endeavor, we address the question of *who*.

Who in the Library?

A program of library and information services requires someone in charge, someone to make short- and long-range plans, to oversee daily operations, and to ensure that the library's collection and services are responsive to the needs of the museum community. Ideally, this person is degreed in library and information science; in the real world, other situations occur.[16] And herein we have

> [t]he most serious and widespread handicap [for museum libraries], the non-professional status of the staff.... The management of museum libraries is too often entrusted as a sideline to a museum curator or a secretary, who knows nothing of basic documentary techniques and is unaware of the need to conform to international standards.[17]

This reality, of course, stems from resources—their lack or their allocation. In consequence, the head of one of the museum departments or one of its staff member becomes the titular librarian, and often because that person perceives the need and provides the impetus for a museum library. My 1994 and 1999 research projects suggest that support for the library comes from curators (19 percent and 27 percent, respectively) and administrators (17 percent and 13 percent);[18] not surprisingly, when archivists are on staff, they are involved.[19]

Usually paraprofessional museum staff or volunteers work under the direction of the titular library director. This arrangement is logical enough. It should not mean, however, that the library's collection and services are limited to the needs of the department represented by the staff member who wears the library director's hat from time to time. Moreover, when museum curators, educators, registrars or other staff who assume or are given library oversight do not have library and information science credentials, they need to seek professional counsel and advice, supplemented with a book such as this.

Museum members can be strong advocates for the library and can often take the library's case to the board and administration. They can also undertake much of the preliminary research. Their networks and connections can be invaluable: volunteers know volunteers in other agencies and other places. Given the opportunity to participate in the planning, volunteers prove themselves to be energetic and effective supporters and backers of library collections and places.

They may also be willing library workers under the direction of museum staff or under their own steam. The cautionary note regarding the latter situation is the possibility that such activity may lead, by default more than by design, to one of the least satisfactory arrangements: a committee of volunteers running the library with little or no coordination or consultation with museum staff. There are successful exceptions, certainly, but it is difficult for a volunteer committee to provide much beyond collection and housekeeping or to respond coherently to museum staff needs. Without staff guidance, the "library committee" often does what its members want to do, rather than what needs doing, and concentrates on housekeeping to the exclusion of planning and services.

If the committee chairperson is a librarian, or even if the committee has such a person on call, the library's focus will extend beyond the basic housekeeping and storage chores. Some museums secure full-time or part-time volunteer professionals—retired, perhaps, or not practicing for the time being—and if their knowledge and skills are up to date and the museum treats them as staff, the library reaps the rewards.

In larger museums—and especially if the library has a long history within the parent organization—the library may be a separate department, on an administrative level with other departments, with a professional librarian in charge. Indeed, such an arrangement is the ideal if the resources and personnel for effective operation are available. Very large museums usually have one or more full-time, salaried professional librarians, plus other staff as needed.

Finding the Library's Role

We have taken up the essential questions about the museum library—namely the *what*, *why*, *where*, *how*, and *who*. Next we consider a set of terms and concepts from the fields of organizational behavior and management. Because of their direct bearing on the development and administration of the museum library (or of any entity which is part of another, larger organization and which serves it), these concepts are integral to the start-up and revitalizing phases.

Mission, Goals, Objectives

Plainly put, an organization's *mission* is its reason for being. A history museum, for example, may take the following statement as its mission: "To collect, preserve, and interpret artifacts related to the pottery industry in Mission Valley." Another museum, in a very similar situation, might see its mission as "collecting, preserving and exhibiting bluestone salt glaze pottery." The object collections and exhibits of these museums will differ. And because the role of the special library is to reflect the mission of the parent organization, their libraries also will differ in collections and information services.

To activate the mission, the museum board and staff select several *goals*, or concrete statements of intention. The first museum, then, might adopt as a goal "to achieve a complete type collection from the Smith Family pottery in Mission

Valley." Based on the goals, the museum staff institutes *objectives*, or project-like activities that are specific, doable, measurable, and set in a limited time frame. Out of the Smith Family pottery goal the staff might articulate an objective: "During July and August an intern will search extant pottery records for names or marks of types or patterns of Smith Family production not represented in the collection." This statement, characteristic of well-designed objectives, is *specific* (limited to one pottery), *doable* (using available records), *measurable* (the results of the search can be compared with—measured against—the known pottery in the collection), and *time-framed*, limited to a predetermined length of time (July–August).

These three administrative concepts—mission, goals, and objectives—have an immediate impact on the museum library and information services. The role of the special library within the parent organization is not just to reflect the mission, but also to support the goals and facilitate the achievement of objectives. Hence, the library in our example will already have resources related to Mission Valley and its pottery industry (reflecting the mission) and also materials about the Smiths and their operation (supporting that goal.) To facilitate the objective, the library—in cooperation with the curator—may secure, copy, or locate pottery records, mark and pattern data, and auction or sale records, all before the beginning of the summer internship period.

We see, then, that if the library (or any other museum function or department) is to support the museum, museum and library staff must be very clear about the organizational mission and goals; otherwise the library is apt to go off in one direction, and the museum it serves in another. In fact, one of the major reasons for the failure of special libraries is a lack of congruence between the goals of the organization and the goals of the library.

The pay-off is the special library's wonderfully workable and simple credo:

The library supports the mission and goals of the museum and contributes to its objectives.

While this statement is not intended as a mantra, adherence to its principles solves many questions and issues of management, collections, and services before they are raised. For example, if the museum is dedicated to preserving and interpreting the evidences of the historical development of the local pottery industry, the library cannot be expected to include astronomy books, however useful they might be for science fair projects. The observance of such a statement also demonstrates to museum management the intended role of the library in the life and work of the museum.

The same credo determines library and information services. The library in our example will own or subscribe to data resources such as the "American Life" online file or *Dictionary of Ceramics Engineering*, but not to *Oceanic*

Abstracts. Likewise, the library staff will be ready to provide data and information about salt glazes or about the county's ethnic population, but not about mass transportation (unless it was a factor in the local history or economy).

Krystyna Wasserman, in describing the relationship of the library to the National Museum of Women in the Arts, sees the library's main task (i.e., mission) as providing "information on art by women," with three objectives (i.e., goals) growing from that mission:

- Service to the museum staff and docents
- Service to external clientele
- Service as a depository of the museum publications, as well as publications concerning the museum, its development, collection activities, and programs[20]

This principle of supporting the museum's mission and goals greatly simplifies decision-making for the museum librarian, who can use the principle to settle issues not only of collection development and information service, but also housekeeping details such as hours, loan policies, and collection organization.

In Summary

To bring a library into being, those heading the effort must see that a number of events occur, meetings take place, and ideas evolve and focus. For the library committee eager to get started putting books on the shelves, these preliminaries probably will seem tedious and even tendentious; however, just as careful spadework precedes planting and harvest, so must preparation and planning and the cultivation of financial and moral support for the library precede the big ribbon-cutting. The following lists recapitulate the steps to be taken.

Starting Up

1. A person or persons—ideally an enthusiastic group under strong leadership and with guidance from a library professional—perceive a need and undertake the responsibilities (and adventures) of establishing or reactivating the museum's library. In preparing the case for the library, they research other museum libraries, gather examples from the literature,

query the museum staff regarding their information needs, and tap into their own networks.

2. As part of preparing the library's case, they develop a mission statement and set of goals for the library based on those of the museum. They may even write one or two readily attainable preliminary objectives as demonstration projects.

3. They locate and negotiate for a library location.

4. They present their findings to the museum board and administration.

5. They secure funding: a start-up allocation or grant, plus budget projections for several years; or an annual budget. Whatever the initial mechanism, the library needs assured fiscal support from the museum, and the library should administer its own budget rather than exist as a line item in the budget of another department.

6. They begin the collection, as outlined in chapter 2.

Revitalizing

1. As above.

2. As above.

3. They evaluate the present location of the library (see chapter 3), and either make plans for refurbishing or up-grading the site or negotiate for another location.

4. As above.

5. As above.

6. They evaluate the collection in light of the mission and goals, then plan the collection as in chapter 2.

Notes

1. David Carr, "Minds in Museums and Libraries: The Cognitive Management of Cultural Institutions," *Teachers College Record* 93/1 (Fall 1991): 6–27.

2. Peter Homulos, "Museums to Libraries: A Family of Collecting Institutions," *Art Libraries Journal* 15/1 (1990): 11–13.

3. John Bentley, "An Open Book," *History Today* 48/8 (August 1998): 29–30. Bentley notes that the new British Library carries on the "cabinet tradition" of the old, library melding books and object.

4. American Association of Museums (AAM), *Museums for a New Century* (Washington, D.C.: AAM, 1984).

5. *Museums Count: A Report by the American Association of Museums* (Washington, D.C.: AAM, 1994). This report reframes the data from the AAM publication *Data Report from the 1989 National Museum Survey*. It does not mention libraries among museum facilities, but does include "library services" among public services such as tours, special lectures, and "special events like fairs and festivals" (p. 61).

6. Esther Green Bierbaum, "Museum Libraries: The More Things Change...," *Special Libraries* 87/2 (Spring, 1996): 74–87. Out of more than 100 questions on the AAM's institutional evaluation form, only six apply to the library, and four of these inquire after the organization of the library collection, leaving two questions directed to the library's support of research.

7. Bierbaum, "Museum Libraries," p. 76. The 1999 results are unpublished at this writing.

8. John A. Moorman, *Managing Small Library Collections in Businesses and Community Organizations: Advice for Nonlibrarians* (Chicago: American Library Association, 1989), p. 2.

9. For more information about special libraries and the Special Libraries Association, view the SLA Website: http://www.sla.org.

10. Museum library budgets are not munificent. Forty-five percent of those surveyed reported budgets of less than $1,500, excluding salaries; 5 percent voluntarily noted that "under $1,500" meant zero. See Bierbaum, "Museum Libraries," p. 77.

11. For useful suggestions for grants, see Peggy Barber and Linda D. Crowe, *Getting Your Grant: A How-To-Do-It Manual for Librarians* (New York: Neal-Schuman, 1993).

12. Krystyna Wasserman, "Library and Research Center (LRC) of the National Museum of Women in the Arts (NMWA)," *Art Documentation* 7/1 (Spring 1988): 29; see also Dwight F. Burlingame, ed., *Library Fundraising: Models for Success* (Chicago: American Library Association, 1995), chapter 1, "Endowed Book Funds," pp. 1–12.

13. Odile Tarrête, "Hidden Treasures: Museum Libraries and Documentation Centres." *Museum International*, No. 195, 49/3 (July/Sept, 1997): 43–48.

14. For some specific suggestions, see David R. Worlock, "Implementing the Information Audit," *Aslib Proceedings* 39 (September 1987): 255–260.

15. As an example of support from the literature, see Neil Kotler, "Delivering Experience: Marketing the Museum's Full Range of Assets," *Museum News* 78/3 (May/June 1999): 30–39; 58–61. Kotler cites the library as a means of "increasing a visitor's awareness and knowledge" and as part of the greater variety of "recreation and diversion" offered by museums (p. 39).

16. The Special Libraries Association (SLA), back in 1964, maintained in a pamphlet, "Objectives for Special Libraries," that "the professional librarian is the single most important element in the effective library." The 1990s expression of this sentiment is found in the report "Competencies for Special Librarians of the 21st Century": "In the information age, special librarians are essential." The museum board and administration should be aware of library standards and committed to working toward them. An executive summary of "Competencies" may be viewed at the SLA website: http://www.sla.org/conf/pcp/proder.htm (accessed August 2000).

17. Tarrête, "Hidden Treasure," p. 44.

18. Bierbaum, "Museum Libraries," p. 79.

19. Interestingly, before computers became common in registrars' and curators' departments, museum educators were the leading proponents of the museum library. See Bierbaum, "The Museum Library," p. 112–113.

20. Wasserman, "Library and Research Center," p. 29.

Further Reading

Libraries, Museums, Archives

Alexander, Edward P. *Museums in Motion*. Nashville, Tenn.: American Society for State and Local History (AASLH), 1979.

American Association of Museums (AAM). "Constitution and Bylaws. Adopted June 1, 1976; amended March, 1991." *Museum News* 70/5 (September/October 1991): 90–93.

_____. *Data Report from the 1989 National Museums Survey*. Washington, D.C.: AAM, 1992.

_____. *Museum Accreditation: A Handbook for the Institution*. Washington, D.C.: AAM, 1990.

Bain, Alan L. "The Muses' Memory." *Museum News* 70/6 (November/December 1991): 36–39.

Boyd, Willard L. "Museums as Centers of Learning." *Teachers' College Record* 94/4 (Summer 1993): 761–770.

Burcaw, G. Ellis. *Introduction to Museum Work*. 3rd ed. Nashville, Tenn.: American Association for State and Local History (AASLH), 1997.

Dana, John Cotton. "The Evolution of the Special Library." In *Libraries: Addresses and Essays*, pp. 243–259. New York: H.W. Wilson, 1916.

_____. "Libraries and Museums." *Library Journal* 46 (15 June 1921): 539–540.

_____. *A Plan for a New Museum: The Kind of Museum It Will Profit a City to Maintain*. Woodstock, Vt.: Elm Tree Press, 1920.

Dearstyne, Bruce W. *The Archival Enterprise: Modern Archival Principles, Practices, and Management Techniques*. Chicago: American Library Association (ALA), 1993.

Fleckner, John A. "Archives and Museums." *Midwestern Archivist* 15/2(1990): 67–73.

Guthe, Carl E. *The Management of Small History Museums*. Nashville, Tenn.: AASLH, 1964; 2nd ed., 5th printing, 1982.

Hartt, Kathleen. "A Manifold Resource." *Museum News* 70/6 (November/December 1991): 40–45.

Homulos, Peter. "Museums to Libraries: A Family of Collecting Institutions." *Art Libraries Journal* 15/1 (1990): 11–13.

Mount, Ellis, and Renée Massoud. *Special Libraries and Information Centers: An Introductory Text*. 4th ed. Washington, D.C.: Special Libraries Association (SLA), 1999.

Sager, Donald J. *Small Libraries: Organization and Operation*. Ft. Atkinson, Wis.: Highsmith Press, 1993.

Smith, Ruth S. *Setting Up a Library: How to Begin or Begin Again*. Bryn Mawr, Pa.: Church and Synagogue Library Association, 1979.

Swinney, H. J., ed. *Professional Standards for Museum Accreditation: The Handbook of the Accreditation Program of the American Association of Museums.* Washington, D.C.: AAM, 1978.

Thompson, John M. A., ed. *Manual of Curatorship: A Guide to Museum Practice.* London: Butterworths, 1984.

Tolles, Bryant F., ed. *Museum Curatorship: Rhetoric vs. Reality.* Proceedings of the Eighth Museum Studies Conference, April, 1987. Newark, Del.: University of Delaware, 1987.

Watkins, Charles Allen, "Are Museums Still Necessary?" *Curator* 37/1 (1994): 25–35.

Weil, Stephen E. *Rethinking the Museum, and Other Meditations.* Washington, D.C.: Smithsonian Institution Press, 1990.

Libraries in Museums

Katz, William A., ed. *The How-To-Do-It Manual for Small Libraries.* New York: Neal-Schuman: 1988.

Bierbaum, Esther Green. "Museum Libraries: The More Things Change..." *Special Libraries* 87/2 (Spring 1996): 74–87.

_____. "The Museum Library Revisited." *Special Libraries* 75/2 (April 1984): 102–113.

Kaser, David. *The Library in the Small Historical Society.* Rev. ed. Nashville, Tenn.: AASLH, 1972. (Technical Leaflet no. 27).

Larsen, John C., ed. *Museum Librarianship.* Hamden, Conn.: Library Professional Publications, 1985.

Lipton, Barbara. "The Small Museum Library: The Experience of the Newark Museum Library." *Special Libraries* 65/1 (January 1974): 1–3.

Matthews, Julia. "From Archaeology to Zoology: The ROM Library." *Canadian Library Journal* 43/3 (June 1986): 187–190.

Moorman, John A. *Managing Small Library Collections in Businesses and Community Organizations: Advice for Nonlibrarians.* Chicago: ALA, 1989.

Root, Nina J. "Role of the Museum Library." In Rhoda S. Ratner, ed., *The Role of the Library in a Museum: Session Proceedings, Joint Annual Meeting, American Association of Museums/Canadian Museums Association*, Boston, Massachusetts, June 1980, pp. 4–7. Washington, D.C.: Smithsonian Institution, 1980.

_____. "Biography of a Museum Library." *Curator* 26/3 (September 1983): 185–198.

Tarrête, Odile. Hidden Treasure: Museum Libraries and Documentation Centres." *Museum International*, No. 195, 49/3 (1997): 43–48.

Wasserman, Krystyna. "Library and Research Center (LRC) of the National Museum of Women in the Arts." *Art Documentation* 7/1 (Spring 1988): 29.

Will, Leonard. "Museums as Information Centres." *Museum International*, No. 181, 46/1 (1996): 2025.

Chapter 2

On the Shelves:
Developing the
Library Collection

The print and nonprint materials the museum library organizes and makes accessible constitute the library collection. Acquiring the books and other items, planning and shaping the collection so that it supports the museum's mission, undertaking the steps by which materials are integrated into the collection—these activities are all part of collection management, the subject of this chapter.

First we will examine the philosophy of collection development in the museum library, then procedures for acquiring materials, beginning with ordering an item. Incorporating the item into the collection is the subject of chapter 3; bringing item and reader together, of chapter 6. These processes are similar in purpose to the museum's accessioning, registering (documenting), and cataloging.[1]

The special library also locates or provides materials which are not in the physical collection but which can be accessed by such means as interlibrary loan (ILL) or electronic text services. These and other information services will be described in chapters 6 and 7.

In this chapter we address as "librarian" the someone in charge of the library project and its beginnings; as we have already noted, that someone often wears another hat.

Like the museum, the special library in the museum carries out several general functions directly related to its collection. The library caretakers must

acquire and collect appropriate materials, whether print, nonprint, or—when feasible—electronic;

describe and organize these materials so that they can be stored and retrieved from storage;

provide information and information services based on the collection and according to the needs of the clientele;

furnish instruction in the use of media and materials, print and nonprint bibliographic sources such as the library's catalog, and online resources such as databases and the Internet; and

conserve and preserve the encoded records of human thought and endeavor for future use, including use that may not yet be known.

Libraries do not stress these functions equally. Corporate special libraries, for example, often stress the third function (providing information) and de-emphasize the fourth (instruction), while public libraries may not give much emphasis to preservation (the fifth.) The first two functions, however—acquisition and organization—are the groundwork upon which the other library functions stand.

Collection Development
and Management

As we have noted, almost every museum harbors the beginnings of a library collection. Books and journals can be found on shelves in offices, workrooms, and back halls, in boxes and cabinets, in nooks and crannies; they make up the lurking library. The materials may even be the neglected personal property of staff present or long gone. The library of the Royal Ontario Museum (ROM), for example, began with the private libraries of the curators of a half-century and more ago.[2]

Generally, some of the materials may have been purchased in support of an exhibit or project; others might be gifts from different people on various occasions. And sometimes materials appear to have floated in, mysteriously, on some bibliographical west wind.

Even though the items do not all necessarily relate to the museum's mission, exhibits, or educational programming, at some point in the history of the materials someone on the museum's staff may have attempted to organize them by topic, date, or author, so that they functioned as an informal library collection.

Indeed, this arrangement may suit the staff quite nicely—right up until an information crisis bogs down the developmental stages of a new exhibit.

Ideally, the librarian casts a net throughout the museum's departments and nooks and crannies, assesses each item thus recovered against the library's collection development policy (described in the next section), and retains or discards it. The reality is often more convoluted and less straightforward; the response to these actions can be territorial, with some museum staff members reluctant to give up the books and other items which have lined their shelves—museum property or not.

Their reluctance may stem from what Davenport calls *information politics*, a phenomenon he discusses in terms of corporate culture, but which is also familiar in the not-for-profit setting as an element of turf and competitiveness. The librarian comprehends better than most that information is power, that books and other materials, as carriers of information, symbolize that power. Hence: "When information is the primary unit of organizational currency, we should not expect its owners to give it away."[3]

When the librarian encounters such resistance, rather than antagonize a museum staff member and jeopardize the library's future ability to serve that area or department, discretion becomes the better part of planning. The librarian, as a student of the organization, must be aware of institutional and information politics as elements of the institutional landscape.

It is more effective in the long run to make a bibliographic notation of the items for inclusion in the catalog, but to leave them in place, perhaps as a permanent loan. Nothing is lost and everything is gained by such accommodation; the existence and location of the item are known and the humanity of the librarian is affirmed.

Collection Development Policies

Special library collections are built with an eye toward supporting the parent institution, and the *collection development policy* serves as a blueprint of sorts.

The first task in starting a museum library is to write this collection development policy, whether there are absolutely no resources, or the books are jumbled in a box under the stairs, or even when there are shelves and some semblance of order. In preparing to write the policy, the librarian or group in charge of the library will find guidance by examining the policies of similar libraries. Library science textbooks in collection development also include model policies, although some may be more extensive than the small museum initially requires. (A fictional policy is given in Appendix B to help get the policy ball rolling.) Final preparation should be in consultation with museum staff,[4] and they, along with the administration, need to understand and consent to it.

Collection development policies generally follow a pattern. First, the policy states that the collection supports the mission and goals of the parent institution. Then there comes a declaration of format and the subject matter that will be collected, including any necessary clarification regarding depth and manner of treatment, type of works (such as reference materials, scholarly journals, or unretouched photographs), and acceptable range of publication date.

The policy should also cover sources of acquisitions recommendations, the acceptance of gifts, and the determination of acquisition priorities. It is also wise to include a statement about weeding out irrelevant or out-dated materials, particularly in a scientific collection or if there have been packrat tendencies in the past.

The collection development policy can be used right away to evaluate the materials already on hand in that lurking library. The librarian should not be surprised if the ratio of keepers to discards is low. After all, the materials now being measured by the new standards were generally acquired piecemeal or with a short-term purpose in mind. This initial evaluation exercise also serves as an object lesson in the power of the museum mission to shape the library and information functions.

Then comes a checklist of *materials to include*. It might look like this:

- Books, serials, and materials for the *museum professional*, including administrators

- Books, serials, and materials in the *subject emphasis* of the museum, including reference works, report literature, and monographs but usually not textbooks unless they are the only or most appropriate resource available

- *Guides to the literature* of the museum's subject or discipline. More extensive in treatment than bibliographies, such guides help relate the discipline and its literature to the wider universe of knowledge

- A range of *subject interests* and reading and comprehension levels, if the collection is open to members or the public. Sometimes good children's works (for example, books by Zim, Asimov, and Helm in the sciences) can serve as helpful introductory works for adults. Shelve them without comment or *J* (for "juvenile") labels and let them speak for themselves

Gifts

Just as the museum receives collections from donors who have undertaken spring cleaning or remembered the museum in estate planning, so the library becomes the beneficiary of book donors. Conditions of library donation must conform to the overall gift policies of the museum, and these terms must be written into the collection development policy. Such conditions may include stipulations regarding perpetual conveyance of title to the library, the right of the library to do with the book what is best for the library, and any special conditions pertaining to the gift (e.g., placing in a special collections area).

There are other considerations pertaining to gifts, especially those of cost. It can, for example, take several hours to sort through boxes of books, which may yield one or two "keepers." Thus time and effort must be weighed against the value of potential acquisitions. Moreover, the same time and resources must be devoted to cataloging and preparing gifts; costs of these processes, depending on the library, are estimated to vary from $5 (with volunteer services, obviously) to $50 or more. *Gifts are not free!*

Finally, beware of boxes. Boxes and their contents should be subject to the same fumigation and quarantine procedures as other museum accessions.

Collection Management

The collection development policy should also take in the broader issue of the *management* of a collection, not simply address the acquisition of a certain number of print and nonprint materials. Consequently, keeping the collection current, useful, and accessible—the lean-and-mean approach—is a high priority. Weeding is the other side of the collection coin, for which the policy should state certain standards of currency, accuracy, relevance, and use.

Use, for example, is not necessarily an absolute criterion for weeding. If the museum has completely changed an element of its mission and abandoned a particular set of objects and research pertaining to them, then the library's supporting materials well may go. But if there has been a local shift in the winds of attention—from, say, backyard astronomy to cosmology—promotion and special displays can help redirect attention back to an important element of the collection.[5]

Collection management also includes shelving and storage, access and circulation, and conservation and preservation, as well as reassessment and weeding. Collection management, as a long-term and on-going concern, is lower on the horizon of the starting-up library than, for example, acquiring a basic reference collection. Still, for the library staff anticipating a long-lived organization, plans for the continuing management of the collection beyond the magic of opening day must be incorporated into the earliest planning (hence our emphasis on reflecting the museum's mission and goals and any changes in them, as well as providing information services keyed to the needs of the museum staff). *Relevance* and *flexibility* become key terms in the management of the collection.

Shelving and storage will be discussed in chapter 4; circulation in chapter 6;

and conservation and preservation more extensively—because they are often part of the library's extended services—in chapter 7.

Conservation and Preservation

Conservation and preservation are important aspects of collection management. Essentially, the terms add up to keeping the items in the collection in a usable state and guarding necessary, valuable or unique items from deterioration.[6]

Such measures as microfilming, binding and repairing materials, controlling the humidity and temperature, and waging war on mold and silverfish are, again, longer-term issues that may not engage the rapt attention of a start-up staff; nevertheless, they are management issues that need to be recognized early on with policies and plans to address them as needed. Conservation and preservation will be discussed at greater length in chapter 7.

Archives

Museums acquire and create several kinds of archives, some of which are the logical interest of the library. The archives associated with the objects in the museum collections—the documents of history, provenance and validation—are customarily the charge of the registrar or curator. When registration facilities are crowded for space and the library is the more secure area or has better climate control, the files of these archives may be stored there but are not regarded as part of the library collection. By their nature, archives are subjects of conservation and preservation efforts.[7]

Archival collections—historical documents, records, and even photographs—which are part of the museum's collections of objects are under the charge of the registrar during accession and then pass to the appropriate curator. This type of collection is found particularly in the historical museum.

Again, if archives are a small portion of the museum collections, or if the library offers better storage conditions, these materials may be kept there but will not constitute an element of the library's collection. This arrangement is less frequent because items properly under curation are likely to be appropriately stored.

Archives as library materials

Special libraries often include archival materials in their collections. Documents, illustrations and photographs, and graphics are among the formats and materials that may enrich or enlarge upon the subject area of the collections. These archives are, of course, the charge of the library and are administered in the same manner as other library materials.

Institutional archives

The museum as a whole and also its departments and functional units will, over time, create archives, the historical records of their development, work, and endeavors. The library's archives are naturally maintained by the library.

But what of other internal documents? Too often the items become scattered, subject to periodic fits of housekeeping, or are allowed to become documentary amoebae, multiplying and retained without plan or evaluation.

The library, acting either as custodian or administrator, is a logical place to assemble all the institutional archives. Even when undertaken gradually and in planned phases, archival organization is no small project, one which should not be assumed by the library without guidance from a consulting archivist if the librarian does not have archival training.[8]

The collection development policy should reflect the museum's archival management decisions. Archives will also be discussed in chapter 7.

Acquisitions: Types of Materials and Media

The collection development policy will cover a number of *formats*—types of carriers of intellectual content—including books, serials, and nonprint.

Books

Inevitably, we tend to think of libraries in terms of books. After all, the very word *library* takes its stem from the Latin *libr-*, which signified "bark" and, by extension, "book." And books are often lovely objects, tangible, unitary, utterly countable and amenable to rational and attractive arrangement.

For the museum library, the selection standards are quite straightforward: subject suitability (that is, "within scope"), accuracy, recency (when currency matters), and (it must be said) affordability. For hard-use items, binding is another consideration. When there is a choice, so is acid-free paper. And while books are frequently given to the library, other materials are a different matter.

Serials

Magazines, journals, and their kin are important library holdings. Bibliographically speaking, serials are defined by the condition of publication: they come out in parts (issues); the parts are designated by numeration, chronology, or both; and the editorial intent is for the serial to go on more or less forever. Usually, also, a predetermined set of issues is from time to time gathered into a volume.

Periodicals are not necessarily paperbound materials. Books can be published periodically (monographic serials, such as annuals and yearbooks); additionally, periodicals now "appear" in microfiche, on computer and CD-ROM diskettes and discs, and as audio tapes. Moreover, many journals, especially in the sciences, are being "published" on the Internet, and available (usually for a subscription fee) for reading or downloading.

While some serials are maintaining both print and nonprint versions, other publications are available only in these latter formats, meaning that the library must acquire the necessary hardware and online capabilities in order to subscribe to them. Such costs are in addition to the subscription, although, of course, the hardware and telecommunication connections will have other uses within the library.

Scholarly journals are important to the research efforts of the staff, their study and interpretation of the museum collections, and the development of educational programs. The journal literature is also invaluable to the library because research results appear in journals one or two years before they are published in books, and consequently journals are the most recent—or only—sources of some data. And, of course, the scholar's urge to report first has led to electronic speeds, even while the validity of the online record is being debated in the halls of academe.

Magazines are generally viewed as more colorful, livelier, and of greater interest than journals. The magazine press in a subject area is an important addition to the library that serves the museum membership or the public. Such titles are more than mere lite reading, too: popular titles such as *Natural History*, *History Today*, and *Discover* publish research articles as well as articles that advance lay understanding in the field. The popular subject-area press also affords the staff many clues to the current interests of the public.

The *report* is a sort of speeded-up journal; the Internet has warped-up the speed. The report literature is widely various; however, the individual report itself is usually narrowly focused and may be published more sporadically than journals and magazines. Reports are an essential aspect of the exchange of information in the sciences and social sciences. In a science-technology center, for example, *NTIS Reports* from the National Technical Information Service might be invaluable, as would *World Population Reports* in an anthropology museum.

Reports more nearly resemble pamphlets and brochures in format, although some are substantial in the number of pages and others come in a newsletter format. Some reports are issued on a regular basis by societies, agencies, research projects, and similar organizations, and may even be numbered sequentially; others appear when research dictates.

The currency of content is the important feature of the report, since research results appear in reports even prior to publication in journals. Increasingly, because of the speed of dissemination, reports are being published in online versions or solely online. Reports are usually discarded after the formal journal article is published.

Newspapers are distinguished by the use of newsprint and by the size of the page. The boundary between some newspaper-like magazines and magazine-style newspapers becomes obscure, if not academic. The main concern is that the choice of titles follows the guidelines of the collection development policy.

Orders and Acquisitions

With the collection development policy as a guide (and it can be modified later, as circumstances change in the museum or the library) and the beginnings of the collection at hand, the librarian is ready to acquire materials for the collection. The money, of course, has to come from somewhere.

As noted in chapter 1, the library budget should be an important part of preliminary planning. (Matters budgetary will be discussed in chapter 5.) At this juncture, however, a gift, a grant, or a special appropriation is a helpful validation of progress and mark of support. The collection lacking such a start-up boost can exhibit discouragingly slow growth.

Ordering library materials, especially books, is a straightforward proposition, although in larger libraries, with thousands of items ordered in a year, the process becomes multilayered and complex. We shall discuss basic ordering procedures for books, periodicals (magazines and journals), government publications, nonprint, audiovisual materials, and computer software.

Acquisitions is the formal term for ordering, acquiring, and paying for library materials. For large academic and public libraries, it is a highly automated process; but, in smaller special libraries—except, perhaps for serials ordered from a vendor—acquisitions involves paper and pen.[9]

Ordering Books

Book purchasing information—the publisher and the price—is customarily provided in reviews and other sources. Addresses of publishers are listed in *Cumulative Book Index* (CBI) and *Books in Print* (BIP). Ordering books currently in publication can be as simple as writing a letter to the publisher, although that procedure can become tedious for both parties to the transaction if the museum library orders more than three or four titles a year.

When—as in the case of establishing or reactivating a collection—the librarian orders a larger numbers of books, using the services of a jobber or vendor will prove more efficient. *The American Book Publishing Record* (*ABPR*) lists jobbers, as do the advertising sections of library publications, and some editions of the *Official Museum Products and Services Directory*. Most vendors supply information about their services at a Web site, or URL (Universal Resource Locator) on the World Wide Web. It is also wise to ask other librarians about their experiences with vendors before making a selection; there are some interesting tales out there from the order wars.

An order to a jobber needs to be preceded by a letter of inquiry on the library's or museum's letterhead asking about minimum order size, frequency, discounts, forms, and procedures for ordering, billing, fulfillment, and cancellations and backorders. Transactions with jobbers are now routinely conducted online from the ordering site. If the library or museum does not have such capability, the librarian must determine whether or not the jobber will handle paper transactions.

The right choice of jobber will relieve the librarian of burdensome details of reordering, follow-ups, and even some selection decisions; but there must also be provision for feed-back from the jobber so that the librarian has order information in a timely fashion.

Depending on the nature of the collection and the volume of acquisition, the jobber can be instructed to make routine purchases in conformity with the collection development policy: the librarian may decide, for example, to purchase all of the titles published by a certain publisher in the field, or the works of a certain author or groups of writers, or all the volumes in a particular series. On the basis of such a *blanket order*, the jobber sends the library all the titles caught in the library's self-described net. Moreover, the books are usually sent *on approval*, which means the librarian may return them to the jobber if they are determined to be out of the library's scope.

The same right of return applies to another automatic acquisition technique, the *profile*. In this case, the librarian and jobber enumerate criteria for acquisition: certain subject areas, languages, reading levels, and publishers (for example, all books published by university presses on canal-building in the 18th century). Few small museum libraries order enough books to warrant automatic orders, except perhaps in the start-up phase; but the savings in time offered by profile ordering make the technique worth considering in the larger institution.

Not all purchases are made from a distance. Local suppliers can often fill more routine book needs. It is also sometimes necessary to make quick purchases to accommodate a sudden need, so an arrangement must be made with the business office for a drawing account or petty cash fund.

There are, of course, online sources of books, and these may be another way of quite promptly securing a few titles at a time. While some online suppliers deal only with in-print titles, others have established out-of-print (o.p.) services and can often supply more obscure titles—but not, of course, in as timely a manner.

Some vendors offer print-on-demand services, the books generated either as photocopies of archivally held titles or called up from a full-text database and printed on a high-speed printer. Books printed under such conditions will naturally be more costly, but, *in extremis*, may well be worth it.

When a book is ordered, a long trail of paper or electronic footprints is begun. This *order record* includes all the bibliographic information available at the time of ordering, plus the order information itself, such as the date, vendor, price, and discount. In the paper environment, multipart order forms, available from library supply houses, are useful because the librarian has several duplicate copies to give to the business office, keep in the library order file, and send to the jobber. The multicopy form can be defeated, however, by vendors who require use of their own forms (a point to clear up at initial negotiations with vendors) or by museum business offices that require use of their purchase order forms. One of the charms of online transactions is the short-circuiting of the paperwork trail, but such shortcuts must be cleared through the persons who, in the end, cut the checks.

Even if the librarian operates in a paper-based world, access to a personal computer means that forms can be printed in-house to suit local circumstances. At the very least, a useful piece of equipment for ordering—and for many other clerical procedures in the library—is an electronic memory typewriter with capability for repetitious copying.

In the paper environment, the *order file* is usually arranged by title, although publisher, author, or subject may also be filing headings. The function of the order record and order file is to show the status of each item as information is received. In the case of online ordering, the order file is maintained electronically, although printouts can be made.

When all goes well, the book is ordered, the order record is filed, the book is received promptly and in good order, the order record is pulled from the file, and the bill is verified for payment. Unfortunately, books go out of print, vendors' warehouses run out of copies, and cancellations and backorders result. (Status reports on cancellations and backorders separate the really great vendor from the hosts of competitors.) And even the best of jobbers sometimes sends the wrong title or edition.

When an order is received, the shipment should be protected from staff predation and the contents carefully checked against the invoice and the individual items against the order records. Each item is then examined for blank pages, broken binding, missing plates, upside down pages, or other defects that warrant rejecting and returning the item. (Many libraries, particularly larger institutions, skip this examination because they believe it is not cost-effective.)

When the librarian has ascertained that the invoice, order form, and item in hand are in agreement, the order form is dated, placed in the book, and the book stamped with the library ownership stamp in a preestablished pattern. (Top and bottom stamps are important; others are usually placed on the title page and front and back boards.) The item then normally goes to the processing station. However, if there is a staff rush for it, the item may be then released to the staff member, with a notation of the loan made on the order record.

Ordering Serials

Much of what has been said about ordering books applies to magazines, journals, and newspapers, as well. Some vendors specialize in magazines; others handle both books and periodicals. If the number of subscriptions carried by the library is large, the librarian may find that the services of a serials vendor are invaluable. What can go wrong with a book order can go wrong four, twelve, or 52 times a year in the case of serial titles. Checking-in, making claims for missing issues, and coordinating subscriptions and billing are tasks requiring close attention to detail and considerable tolerance for frustration. Subscription services are now normally online; inquiry should precede any paper-based orders.

Journals are often ordered through the same jobber as magazines, although there are journal specialists in specific subject areas, languages, countries, and publishers. Some journals can be obtained by order only from the issuing society; many journals have a multi-tiered subscription structure under which the largest libraries pay the most.

Indeed, journal prices are a topic of heated and emotional discussion, particularly among academic and special librarians.[10] The cost of journals has been rising faster than budgets and much faster than inflation, so that many libraries have cut their subscription lists in the last several years, while others are exploring alternative means of providing access to journal literature, a search that has upset the delicate scholar-publisher-vendor-library balance.[11]

Journals are important in the museum library collection, but the decision to acquire journals should be considered carefully and weighed closely against the needs of the library patrons. The librarian must keep in mind the fact that subscriptions are budget encumbrances (which means that money has been spent in advance of receiving goods), and that subscriptions take more time to turn off than to turn on.

It is useful to locate nearby sources of journals in the museum's subject field. College and university libraries and the libraries of corporations and research institutions are often willing to give museum libraries access to their journals, particularly if reciprocity of access to other materials can be offered in return. Gifts of needed journals are welcome, particularly when they come promptly and consistently.

Subscriptions to local newspapers are secured from the newspaper's circulation department. Subject-specific newspapers are obtained either from the publisher or through the museum's periodicals agent.

The report and ephemeral literature (what the British Library aptly calls "the gray literature") is more difficult both to locate and to secure on a continuing basis. The identity of the issuing organization and address can usually be found in a recent copy of the publication. The address of a learned society, association, or agency can also be obtained from directories of associations or subject disciplines.

The librarian should enlist the museum staff's help in procuring reports, preprints, and other ephemeral materials. Staff members often have professional networks (their "invisible college") to cue them into the report literature. In addition, they often attend conferences and professional meetings where such materials are distributed or displayed. The librarian may try to train the museum staff to "bring back one of everything for the library" to build up the report file with significant and useful documents.

Ordering Government Publications

The publications of federal, state, and local governments and agencies are important in many museum library collections. Federal publications vary widely, some existing in audiovisual format, some in computer datafiles. Many of the agencies print lists of their titles, while the *Monthly Catalog*, available by placing the library's name and address on the mailing list, is a more general list of government publications.

Depository libraries, usually large public or university libraries, are an excellent source of bibliographic data about government publications. They also give the museum librarian the opportunity to examine publications prior to ordering.

Some agencies are now maintaining sites on the World Wide Web (WWW) that include bibliographic information about their publications. Federal materials are purchased from the Government Printing Office, with payment by check, subscription, or prepurchased coupons. A number of vendors also provide purchase options for "gov. docs." (government documents).

Similar procedures hold true for bibliographic information about and purchasing of state and local materials.

Acquiring Nonprint and Audiovisual Materials

The museum, in presenting objects to tell its story and fulfill its mission, is itself an audiovisual collection. The exhibits are full of things to look at, often to listen to, and sometimes to touch and handle. But just as print supplements and enhances the presentation of objects, so nonprint sources of information can expand and enhance the museum library's print collection. The museum library, in support of the museum mission, should include film and video, audio, graphic, three-dimensional, and electronic formats.

The acquisition of nonprint formats is not as formalized as the ordering of books and serials; bibliographic control of nonprint materials has not kept up with the proliferation of the media. Suggestions for sources of what we might term "classic" audiovisual materials are listed in the Ellison and Coty title in "Further Reading."

Reviewing media and library periodicals not only evaluate videos, sound recordings and CD-ROMs, but provide sources and addresses. Subject-area bibliographies and the recommendations of staff and colleagues are especially important sources of information about audiovisuals. Acquisition is then usually a matter of ordering the materials directly from the producer or distributor.

Renting or borrowing motion picture films and videos can often be arranged through local sources. Video rentals and retail outlets carry the more popular videos and will sometimes order educational videotapes.

Reputable distributors and producers offer audiovisual materials on approval to librarians (whose professional ethics will limit the use of materials loaned in this way to preview purposes).

Computer software, especially the plug-and-play programs for personal computers, has become increasingly useful in special libraries, and museum librarians need to be alert to the possibilities of this medium. Decision-based games in ecology and human behavior, software programs demonstrating identification and taxonomic keys, self-instruction on all manner of topics, and databases in mathematics, statistics, and chemistry—these and many more computer programs can support various aspects of the museum's programs and thus find their way into the library collection. John Damuth describes "the electronic museum": acquired and locally produced databases which he regards as "non-material research collections," and which librarians will recognize as potentially part of the museum library collections.[12]

CD-ROM (Compact **D**isc, **R**ead-**O**nly **M**emory), the compact disc now favored by audiophiles, has expanded the museum's computer possibilities by transmitting text, graphics and motion to the computer screen; it is expected that DVD (Digital Versatile Disc and Digital Videodisk) will do the same. Bibliographic databases—both for library cataloging and bibliographic data search and retrieval—as well as the full text of encyclopedias, dictionaries, and other reference tools, are now available for purchase or subscription.

Libraries will have other media delights from which to choose in addition to CD and DVD, from CDs that are "writable" (WORM, or write-once-read-many-times) to the interactive media that engage the young and intrigue their elders. In the face of such a dazzling array, the librarian will need disciplined and earnest consultation of the library's collection development policies.

Software selection and purchase is fairly straightforward compared to other nonbook materials. Many computer magazines review software, as do library, education, and audiovisual journals, where sources and addresses are listed should local computer stores and other retailers not carry the program of interest.

Software is usually sold with a licensing agreement stipulating the conditions under which it may be copied and used. Software producers sometimes offer terms for library and educational use, including discounts, licenses for multiple sites or machines, and other special arrangements.

The Internet, with both free and fee software available for the downloading, offers both pleasures and pains. The pleasures include easy accessibility from the library's computer, the opportunity to try something out without intervening transactions at the post office or store, and the thrill of the chase to find the right program. The pains, unfortunately, include the risk of compromising and crashing one's own system, the introduction of viral contagion, and questions of quality.

It is better to be cautious and put off acquisition (while letting a colleague download and try out the software, for instance) than to suffer the costs of a damaged computer system in terms of time, money, and stress. *Free is not without cost!*

Another thorny electronic issue that the museum library will likely have to face—eventually, if not immediately—is the preservation of digital materials, whether as subscriptions to online journals, or texts purchased—and available only—as online or digitized documents. The transmogrification of computer files—*migrating* is the term—from old hardware and operation systems to new is a problem that is not being solved readily.[13]

Once library materials have been acquired, or the processes set up for doing so, and the lurking library has been weeded according to the collection policy, it will be time to turn to the matters of organizing and processing the materials, discussed in chapter 3.

In Summary

After the beginning steps toward a museum library have been taken, the librarian and library staff or committee must then take the next necessary steps to ensure a coherent and useful collection of materials.

Starting-Up

1. The initial task is the writing of a collection development policy. The policy clearly reflects the mission and goals of the museum and the proposed range, scope and, subject matter of the collection. The policy should be reviewed from time to time and revised and rewritten to reflect changing conditions within the museum or the library.

2. The library staff gathers the books, magazines, and nonprint materials found about the museum, evaluates them against the collection policy, and keeps or discards them—more likely the latter.

3. The staff begins the acquisition of materials by

    Setting up a want file—books and other materials needed for the collection in approximate order of priority; and

    Outlining the steps in the order process and the necessary files, paper and electronic;

    Selecting a vendor and trying out an initial order.

Revitalizing

1. As above.

2. Using not only the collection policy but such criteria as condition, recency of use, and availability of newer editions, the staff applies step 2, above to the present collection.

3. As above.

Notes

1. Carl E. Guthe, *The Management of Small History Museums*, 2nd ed. (Nashville, Tenn.: American Association for State and Local History, 1974), pp. 35–37.

2. Julia Matthews, "From Archaeology to Zoology: The ROM Library," *Canadian Library Journal* 43/3 (June 1986): 187–190.

3. Thomas H. Davenport, Robert G. Eccles, and Laurence Prusak, "Information Politics," *Sloan Management Review* 34/1 (Fall 1992): 54.

4. Odile Tarrête, "Hidden Treasure: Museum Libraries and Documentation Centres," *Museum International*, No. 195, 49/3 (1997): 43–48.

5. Andrew Berner, "Library Management Includes Customer Service, a Team Focus—and Library Promotion, Done Subtly," *InfoManagement* 4/12 (November 1977): 1–3.

6. For succinct definitions of these terms, *see ALCTS Newsletter* 1/2 (1990): 14–15: *Conservation* is "the treatment of library or archive [*sic*] materials, works of art, or museum objects to stabilize them physically, sustaining their survival as long as possible in their original form"; *preservation* implies "activities associated with maintaining library, archival or museum materials for use, either in the original physical form or in some other format."

7. Sherelyn Ogden, ed., *Preservation of Library & Archival Materials: A Manual*, rev. and expanded ed. (Andover, Mass.: Northeast Document Conservation Center, 1994.)

8. Elizabeth Yakel, *Starting an Archives* (Chicago: Society of American Archivists, 1994).

9. Richard W. Boss, "Options for Acquisitions," *Library Technology Reports* 33/4 (July-August 1997): 403–495. He emphasizes (p. 490) that the *price* of an acquisition is less important a consideration than its *cost*, which is the price plus whatever else is associated with its procurement.

10. Lee Ketcham–Van Orsdel and Kathleen Born, "Serials Publishing in Flux," *Library Journal* 124/7 (15 April 1999): 48–53. Journal prices have risen more steeply than inflation (see their table 9, p. 52); the average subscription price in the sciences exceeded $618 in 1999, with physics journals topping out at an average cost of $1,717.

11. Ketcham–Van Orsdel, "Serials Publishing," p. 48. There is far more at stake now than described in Rebecca T. Lenzini, "Serials Prices: What's Happening and Why," *Collection Management* 12/1-2 (1990): 21–29.

12. John Damuth, "The Electronic Museum: Non-material Research Collections in Biology and Paleontology," *ASC (Association of Systematics Collections) Newsletter* 17/22 (April 1989): 25–27.

13. Katie Hafner, "Books to Bytes: The Electronic Archive," *The New York Times* (8 April 1999), Section D ("Circuits.")

Further Reading

Collection Development and Management

Berk, Robert A. "Acquiring and Developing the Collection," pp. 63–82. In *Starting, Managing and Promoting the Small Library*. Armonk, N.Y.: M.E. Sharpe, 1989.

Damuth, John. "The Electronic Museum: Non-Material Research Collections in Biology and Paleontology." *ASC* (Association of Systematics Collections) *Newsletter* 17/22 (April 1989): 25–27.

Ellison, John W., and Patricia Ann Coty, eds. *Nonbook Media: Collection Management and User Services.* Chicago: American Library Association (ALA), 1987.

Evans, G. Edward. *Developing Library and Information Center Collections.* 3rd ed. Littleton, Col.: Libraries Unlimited, 1995.

Gensel, Susan, and Audrey Powers. "Collection Development and the Special Library." *Bookmark* 4/11 (Fall 1982): 11–15.

Gray, David P. "A Technique for Manuscript Collection Development Analysis." *Midwestern Archivist* 12/2 (1987): 91.

Keene, Suzanne. *Digital Collections: Museums and the Information Age.* Boston: Butterworth-Heinemann, 1998.

Newman, Wilda B., and Michlean J. Amir. "Report Literature: Selecting Versus Collecting." *Special Libraries* 69/11 (November 1978): 415–424.

Nisonger, Thomas E. *Management of Serials in Libraries.* Englewood, Col.: Libraries Unlimited, 1998.

Ollé, James G. *A Guide to Sources of Information in Libraries.* Brookfield, Vt.: Gower, 1984.

Schroeder, Fred E. H., ed. *Twentieth Century Popular Culture in Museums and Libraries.* Bowling Green, Ohio: Bowling Green University Popular Press, 1981.

Archives

Deiss, William A. *Museum Archives: An Introduction.* Chicago: Society of American Archivists (SAA), 1984.

Ogden, Sherelyn, ed. *Preservation of Library & Archival Materials: A Manual.* Rev. and expanded ed. Andover, Mass.: Northeast Document Conservation Center, 1994.

Pederson, Ann. *Keeping Archives.* Sydney: Australian Society of Archivists, 1987.

Yakel, Elizabeth. *Starting an Archives.* Chicago: SAA; Metuchen, N.J.: Scarecrow Press, 1994.

Representative Bibliographic Sources

Balachandran, Sarojini, ed. *Encyclopedia of Environmental Information Sources: A Subject Guide to About 34,000 Print and Other Sources of Information on All Aspects of the Environment.* Detroit: Gale, 1993.

Hurt, Charlie. *Information Sources in Science and Technology.* 3rd ed. Englewood, Col.: Libraries Unlimited, 1998.

McClung, Patricia, ed. *Selection of Library Materials in the Humanities, Social Sciences, and Sciences.* Chicago: ALA, 1985.

McCrank, Lawrence J. "Bibliographic Services of the American Historical Association: Recently Published Articles and Writings on American History." A report of the ABH/AHA Task Force, 1989. ERIC: ED312200.

Norton, Mary Beth, and Pamela Gerardi, ed. *The American Historical Association's Guide to Historical Literature.* 3rd ed. New York: Oxford University Press, 1995.

Prucha, Francis Paul. *Handbook for Research in American History: A Guide to Bibliographies and Other Reference Works.* Lincoln, Neb.: University of Nebraska Press, 1987.

Prytherch, Raymond John. *Information Management and Library Science: A Guide to the Literature*. Aldershot, Hants (England); Brookfield, Vermont: Gower, 1994.

Sable, Martin H, ed. *Research Guides to the Humanities, Social Sciences, Sciences and Technology: An Annotated Bibliography of "True Guides" to Library Resources and Usage, Arranged by Subject or Discipline of Coverage*. Ann Arbor, Mich.: Pierian, 1986.

Shapiro, Beth J., and John Whaley, ed. *Selection of Library Materials in Applied and Interdisciplinary Fields*. Chicago: ALA, 1987.

Special Libraries Association. *Tools of the Profession*. 2nd ed. Washington, D.C.: SLA, 1991.

Walker, Richard D., and C. D. Hurt. *Scientific and Technical Literature: An Introduction to Forms of Communication*. Chicago: ALA, 1990.

Webb, William H. *Sources of Information in the Social Sciences: A Guide to the Literature*. 3rd ed. Chicago: ALA, 1986.

Chapter 3

Technical Services:
Organizing the Collection

Just as museum registrars must be able to produce on demand an object or its certified location, or a set of objects which are related in a prescribed way, so must the librarian be able to locate an item in the collection, a group of items having a common characteristic, or a set of data. The array of activities that support the ability to locate carriers of information are lumped together as *technical services*. Broadly speaking, they encompass the processes and activities that make it possible for the library staff to place an item in the hands of the reader, and so may even include circulation.

The aids maintained by technical services—the files, the catalog, and the shelf arrangement—are intended to be intuitive and self-explanatory to the library patron, although the underlying activities are anything but. Technical services somewhat uneasily inhabit an area of library management filled with contradictions: the organization of the collection is the intellectual heart of information services, yet it also is the activity most frequently hung with the musty-fusty image. The organization of the collection is the function often most in need of professional direction, yet its steps include activities that are routine and clerical. Unlike reader services, which include personal interactions, technical services remain largely occult and occluded as far as the reader's perceptions go; but those processes and activities make it possible to locate reference help or consult the catalog or check out materials. Hence, **technical services are also reader services**.

Technical services, labor-intensive as it is, is also a visibly costly operation.

As a precautionary measure, the library staff can be armed with some figures comparing savings in museum staff time *vs.* cataloging costs, and cataloging costs *vs.* replacement costs of "misplaced" items. Moreover,

> **[e]ffective reference service depends on quality cataloging.** The local catalog is a library's single most important reference tool, because it answers users' questions about the collection.[1]

Another issue that often arises in connection with costs is that of *out-sourcing*, lately a topic of extensive discussion in the library literature.[2] It is unlikely that the starting-up museum library will have the sustained volume of acquisitions—and hence, of cataloging—to attract an outside service. The revitalizing library, however, faced with a large recataloging project, might consider a one-time, short-term contract.

Once the collection occupies more than a dozen shelves, cupboards, or drawers, the identity and location of a specific item or a group of items cannot be carried in the librarian's head; a consistent system for identifying and locating library materials must be used, a system that is familiar to users, and one that can grow and develop with the collection. Adherence to a carefully constructed set of technical standards and processes helps ensure a functionally sound library and information service.

The next sections of this chapter discuss technical services under two headings: first, the *organization* of the collection; second, the *preparation* of items for use. Our discussion is based largely on the paper files and manual methods that museum libraries most often use in the beginning.[3] However, the principles underlying the processes remain the same in the electronic, computerized environment; only the methodologies and some of the appearances are altered. Use of, or conversion to, electronic processes is more fully discussed in chapter 8.

Organization

Organization is composed of two distinct but closely related activities: *description*, which is the creation of the elements (or records) in a catalog; and *classification*, which is the location of items relative to one another in terms of subject-matter. Many text books refer to these activities under the rubric of "cataloging," an activity then divided into "descriptive cataloging" (the creation of the bibliographic records in the catalog) and "subject cataloging" (the classification and subject organizing function). "Description and organization" is another term for cataloging.

Organization, then, denotes the activities that create *bibliographic access* to an item; the activities which ensure *physical access*, or readiness for use, are *preparation*, or processes. In using these terms we shall try to avoid confusion with the museum use of the same or similar terms: accession, catalog, and classification. The library connotation will be assumed unless museum use is stated.

As noted earlier, accession and registration in the museum (that is, entering an object into the collection) are, taken together, roughly equivalent to descriptive cataloging and organization in the library; and museum cataloging (the creation of the object catalog or catalogs) is similar to library subject cataloging.

Description: Creating Catalog Records

The museum registrar creates *surrogates* for the objects in the collection—that is, records that stand in for the objects. Once upon a time the records were entered in books. They are now sometimes entered on cards but more often, especially in larger museums, in computer databases. So also the librarian creates surrogates, or records for the items and materials in the library.

These *bibliographic records*—when on cards—are filed alphabetically to create the library's *catalog*. One item will have several records filed in various places in the catalog. These places, called entries or *access points*, permit the item to be looked for in various ways within the same catalog—by author, by title, by subject—without changing the shelf or file location of the item being sought. Consequently, the bibliographic record contains two important data sets: one, unambiguously describing the item; the other, symbolizing the location of the item in the collection.

The content and arrangement of the descriptive data is governed by a set of cataloging rules, *Anglo-American Cataloguing Rules*, 2nd edition, in its 1988 revision, popularly known as AACR2R and AACR2 rev., and jointly published by the American Library Association, the Canadian Library Association, and the (British) Library Association.[4] The AACR2 follows the bibliographic patterns formulated in the *International Standard Bibliographic Description*, or *ISBD*.

All these acronyms sound more formidable than they actually are. Libraries do not **have** to use AACR2 to produce bibliographic records; some do not. The Library of Congress does not send inspectors around to find out. However, as libraries have exchanged more and more bibliographic information through databases, interlibrary loan, and cooperative programs, the AACR2 standard has become the norm. Thus, if the librarian plans to use the *CIP* (Cataloging in Publication) information in books, or the commercially prepared catalog copy available from vendors and online bibliographic utilities, it is sound advice to begin with the AACR2 format, so that the catalog is uniform from the beginning, with the records in standard format.

The AACR2 makes it possible to describe *all* formats and carriers of information and intellectual content in a single, consistent manner. The data elements that make up the description always appear in the same order and are preceded by the same nonsemantic, stylized punctuation. The template also means that the local catalog records describe all media in the same manner, and that bibliographic records for serials, films, audiotapes, and computer software not only appear in the catalog, but are described according to the same conventions.

Further, the communications format for the online, electronic exchange of bibliographic records, **MARC** (**Ma**chine **R**eadable **C**ataloging), reflects in its fields and subfields the same areas into which the bibliographic data are ordered and organized in AACR2 and ISBD. The computer format will be discussed more fully in chapter 8; in this chapter we look more closely at the paper-based catalog and its printed records.

Unlike museum catalogs, in which the records may be structured differently for different files (such as Donor, Location, Insurance, Topic, and so forth), library catalogs have records that are uniform and invariant except for the datum recorded in the topmost (i.e., filing) line. Thus the ISBD/AACR2 structure serves all locations in the library catalog. (See Appendix C for a fuller explanation of this structure.)

The basics of bibliographic description are not difficult to comprehend. The first step is to create the *unit record* (once known, for reasons past and over, as the "main entry.") The heading on this card is usually—but not always!—the name of the author or creator of the item in hand, that name recorded in its *authorized form*.

This form of the name is not necessarily the one on all title pages. Peter J. Somename may use, in various writings, P. J. Somename, Pete Somename, and Peter Somename. However, all the library's holdings will appear under *Somename, Peter J.*, which serves as the *primary, or principal, access point* to the bibliographic information about any of his writings. This bringing together related records at one access point is *collocation*.

We can think of this primary access card as the master record for that item. From it are created the other cards that lead the reader to the item by way of its title, its subject matter, or its alternative title. Right now, on a rectangle of paper about 3 inches by 5 inches, we can construct a description of this book, following the instructions in Appendix C. The final product—the unit record and primary access—should look like this:

Bierbaum, Esther Green.
    Museum librarianship / Esther Green
Bierbaum.—2nd ed.—Jefferson, N.C. :
McFarland, 2000.
    x, 189 pp. : ill. ; 25 cm.

    Includes bibliographical references and
index.
    ISBN 0-7864-0867-7

    1. Museum libraries. 2. Special libraries.
3. Museums—Information services.
I. Title.

Figure 3.1: Primary access record ("main entry") *(Note: The author is not always the main entry; corporate names and even titles can be main entries, as AACR2 indicates in Rules 21.1B2 and 21.1C. Author name is the most common primary access, however.)*

The alert reader will recognize that the record just created bears a strong resemblance to the CIP record on the back of this book's title page. No cause for wonder; they are both based on the same standard, AACR2.

This bibliographic record will also be filed under the other access points (also called added entries), which are listed in the *tracings* at the bottom of the card. In the tracings section of the record, subjects are listed first in Arabic numbering in the order of importance; nonsubject entries (in this case, "I. Title.") follow, designated by Roman numbers. Thus every entry shows all the access points.

To create the additional entries, the access points are added to the main entry record above the primary entry. The top portion of the title entry for this book will look like Fig. 3.2 at the top of page 44.

A computer catalog, or online public access catalog (*OPAC*), however, would probably label the areas of data as in Fig. 3.3 (see page 44). This record will consistently come up on the screen, whether the reader asks for it by author, title, or subject.

Copy Cataloging: Finding Catalog Records

The days when librarians did their own thing in their own unique catalogs have been—mercifully!—superseded by cooperative cataloging. Librarians now do *derived*, or *copy*, cataloging, locating the text of the bibliographic unit record—the primary access record—from which to create the card set for a

Museum librarianship.
Bierbaum, Esther Green.
    Museum librarianship / Esther Green
Bierbaum.—2nd ed.—Jefferson, N.C. :
McFarland, 2000.
    x, 189 pp. : ill. ; 25 cm.

Figure 3.2: Truncated record, showing title access point, or title added entry.

Auth.:	Bierbaum, Esther Green.
Title:	Museum librarianship /
Edition:	2nd ed.
Place:	Jefferson, N.C.
Publshr:	McFarland
Date:	2000.
Descrp.:	x, 189 pp. : ill. ; 25 cm.
Subj.:	Museum libraries
Subj.:	Special libraries
Subj.:	Museums—Information services
Note:	Includes bibliographical references and index.
ISBN:	0000000

Figure 3.3: Fig. 3.1 rendered as a labeled display.

particular item in their collection. The copy cataloger is at liberty to modify the cataloging copy according to local standards and tastes, to add other access points, or to change the classification. Copy cataloging is not a breeze; one must first of all locate copy that exactly matches the item in hand and then modify it as necessary.

Cataloging copy is available for most of the books published in the United States and Canada during the last several decades, and for those published in many other countries as well. Under the CIP program, the publisher submits a book in galley form to the Library of Congress, where a brief record is prepared and returned to the publisher for printing on the verso of the book's title page. This CIP record also becomes available on the tapes made of the bibliographic records of the Library of Congress in electronic form. The *National Union Catalog* (NUC) and *Cumulative Book Index* (CBI) are other sources of primary access copy.

The fly in the bibliographic ointment, of course, is that the library must create a set of records—author, title, and one or more subjects—for each item, or have multiple copies of the main entry produced and the appropriate headings (access points) added at the top. (Here, a memory typewriter is a useful piece of equipment. Computer software programs are also available for card production. See Appendix D.)

Until March 1, 1997, the Library of Congress Cataloging Distribution Service (CDS) sold card sets. Having suspended the service, it now provides a list of commercial producers of cards at its Web site (URL): http://lcweb.loc.gov/cds/cardsl.html.

Online bibliographic utilities such as OCLC (Online Computer Library Center, Inc.) also produce cards. Along with the book order, some book jobbers supply card sets, which must, however, be examined for compatibility with the local catalog. Cataloging data (but not card copy) can also be found at the Library of Congress Web site. (Sources of cataloging copy and catalog cards are also listed in Appendix D.)

While it may no longer be necessary for the librarian to create, one by one, a catalogful of original bibliographic records, it is absolutely necessary for the librarian to have an understanding of the principles of bibliographic description to evaluate and correct cataloging copy.[5] In addition to a copy of AACR2R, the library's professional collection should include a copy of one of the recent cataloging textbooks. Some of the most useful are:

- Lois Mai Chan's second edition of *Cataloging and Classification: An Introduction* (New York: McGraw-Hill, 1994) is well organized and comprehensive.

- Bohdan S. Wynar's standard work, *Introduction to Cataloging and Classification*, edited in the ninth edition by Arlene G. Taylor (Littleton, Colo.: Libraries Unlimited, 2000), deals fully with the cataloging code.

- Susan Gray Akers' *Akers' Simple Library Cataloging*, completely revised and rewritten in the seventh edition by Arthur Curley and Jana Varlejs (Metuchen, N.J.: Scarecrow, 1984), is a very accessible beginner's handbook. It does not provide complete information on cataloging formats other than books, nor does it cover Library of Congress Classification.

- Rosalind E. Miller and Jane C. Terwillegar's *Commonsense Cataloging* (New York: H.W. Wilson, 1990), the revised 4th edition of Esther G. Piercy's *Commonsense Cataloging*, is also good for beginners, but is not comprehensive.

- Mildred H. Downing and David Downing, *Introduction to Cataloging and Classification*, seventh edition (Jefferson, N.C.: McFarland, 1992), is a reasonable compromise between the exhaustive treatment of descriptive cataloging in Wynar and the simplified level of Akers or Miller and Terwillegar.

Classification: Subject Organization

A final piece of data to be included on the bibliographic record is the location of the item in the museum library's collection. In the case of books, the location is usually indicated by a symbol for the subject of the work—hence the term *classification number*. The classification brings works together by broad subject area (such as 973, American History, or 577, Ecology) and then, when discriminations are useful, by subdivisions of the subject (e.g., 973.5, Early 19th Century American History, or 577.7, Marine Ecology.)

American libraries usually use one of the two principal classification systems, the Dewey Decimal Classification (DDC) or the Library of Congress Classification (LCC). The sources for the classification schemes are:

- Melvil Dewey, *Dewey Decimal Classification and Relative Index*, edition 21, edited by Joan S. Mitchell *et al.* (Albany, N.Y.: Forest Press/OCLC, 1996), 4 volumes; also available on CD-ROM; updates at: http://www.oclc.org/fp/.

- Melvil Dewey, *Abridged Dewey Decimal Classification*, 13th edition (Albany, N.Y.: Forest Press/OCLC, 1997).

- Lois Mai Chan *et al.*, *Dewey Decimal Classification: A Practical Guide*, 2nd edition, revised for DDC21 (Albany, N.Y.: Forest Press/OCLC, 1996).

- Library of Congress, Subject Cataloging Division, *Library of Congress Classification: Classes A–Z*, various editions (Washington, D.C.: Library of Congress, 1896–), 40+ volumes.

As the name implies, LCC is a product of the Library of Congress and has been adopted by many large libraries, particularly university and research libraries. It has appeared on cataloging copy sold by the Library of Congress since 1901 and is included today on all Library of Congress MARC (USMARC) cataloging records.

While LCC is not more difficult to learn to use, it is less accessible than DDC for the small library because each class—represented by an alphabetical letter or letters—is published separately and because the system has no overall index or guide to application other than instructions found in subject cataloging textbooks. (There are, however, commercially published indexes available.)

Smaller collections, then, will find the DDC easier to use for the times when classification must be assigned in-house. In addition to the full DDC schedule, the abridged edition is designed for very small collections. Sometimes libraries use the abridged version for all materials except their primary subject area, to which they apply the full Dewey classification. Fortunately, recent MARC records and other sources of cataloging copy usually carry the full DDC designation.

The *call number*, or location symbol, is usually made up of two lines. The first line is the DDC classification; the second is the book number, or a symbol standing for author and title. (The so-called Cutter tables translate names or initial title words into alphanumeric designations.) Consequently, items are arranged not only by subject, but also alphabetically by author within the subject, thus:

027.68	069	069
M87	A38m	B88i

represent, in order, *Museum Librarianship*, edited by Larsen; Alexander's *Museums in Motion*; and Burcaw's *Introduction to Museum Work*.

Not all libraries use DDC or LCC. Many special libraries develop their own classification schemes because of the particular subject or focus of the collection. In addition, subject-specific classification schemes have been published in various subject areas. The best known is the National Library of Medicine (NLM) classification, but there are also classifications for municipal materials (Glidden), petroleum (Uren Decimal), music (Coates/ British Catalogue of Music), school and educational materials (Cheltenham), and business (London), among others.

Some collections and literatures are self-classifying; law was long regarded as a self-classified literature, and many law offices still follow the traditional arrangement by jurisdiction and by court level within jurisdiction. The Government Printing Office also classifies the documents published by agencies and divisions of government.

A locally devised classification may well be adequate while the collection is growing and developing its services, but the staff should keep in mind that a nonstandard organization may confuse the patron who uses other libraries and may also prove to be insufficiently discriminating when the collection grows in size and complexity. Moreover, the advantages of cooperative cataloging are not fully realized unless all of the record data (including classification) are used.

Classification numbers also generally serve as book locators, or call numbers. (When stacks were closed, readers "called for" a title found in the catalog by the shelf locator, which was often the classification—hence the term *call number*.) Bound volumes of journals, cases of filmstrips and videos, boxes of games, and other book-like materials that can be shelved with books can also be located by classification. Other location symbols are used for materials stored in files and drawers, or in a sub-collection. Thus *PROF* or *REF* may be used to designate materials in a professional collection (and perhaps shelved in a staff area) or on reference shelves, while *PICT*, *VID*, or *3D* may be used to indicate the location of pictures, videos, or three-dimensional objects. The location indicator may also be coupled with a classification or an alphabetic or numeric designator. In any case, **no two items in the collection should bear the same call number**. (Thus the need for an accession number is also eliminated.)

Subject Headings and Subject Access

The *subject heading*, or entry, provides subject access with a word or phrase that concisely expresses the "aboutness" of the item. Thus ECOLOGY, or SEASHORE ECOLOGY, or SEASHORE ECOLOGY—GEORGIA are used to describe works of increasing specificity. As previously noted, subject headings are listed under Arabic numerals in the tracings at the bottom of the record.

The terms used in subject headings are taken from a standard *subject headings list* or from a *thesaurus*; they are not made up willy-nilly. Below are the two standard lists most used in libraries:

- Minnie Earl Sears, *Sears List of Subject Headings*, 15th edition, edited by Martha T. Mooney (New York: H. W. Wilson, 1994).

- Library of Congress, Subject Cataloging Division, *Library of Congress Subject Headings*, 23rd edition (Washington, D.C.: The Library, 2000), 5 volumes. The printed version (popularly known as *LCSH* and "Big Red") is now issued annually. The list is sold in microfiche and CD-ROM formats; the electronic tape version, revised daily, is accessible through the major bibliographic utilities such as OCLC and RLIN and on the Internet at: http://lcweb.loc.gov/catdir/cpso/wls.html.

Just as classifications have been developed for specific subject areas, so, too, have subject heading lists for fields such as medicine, and thesauri for education, art, chemistry, engineering, and many other specialties.

While there are technical and structural differences between subject heading lists and thesauri, they both serve the purpose of *vocabulary control* by adhering to a uniform style, choice, and form of terms to be used for subject access. Thus they fulfill the same role in the library catalog as a nomenclature does in the museum catalog.[6] Vocabulary control is the key factor in subject access: the same term is applied to a subject (or aboutness) wherever and whenever it occurs in the collection. (Again, this is the principle of collocation.)

The librarian should examine the various lists and thesauri and select the one most directly applicable to the collection in hand. Additions and modifications can be made when necessary to suit local usage. These changes must be noted in the list so that there is an *authority record*. Using the *Library of Congress Subject Headings* carries the benefit of having the subject headings listed in the MARC record.

To skimp on the detail and care necessary to develop and preserve effective subject access is to invite catalog disaster through a mishmash of headings that hinder and decrease access to items in the collection. Subject access is the only means (other than shelf browsing) to locate an item known only by subject or to secure a group of items dealing with the same subject.

Necessary adjuncts to subject headings and their controlled vocabularies are the *cross-references* placed in the catalog to guide the user from a term he might seek to the term actually used in the catalog. Since *cats* is a perfectly good laymen's term, a zoo library might have a cross-reference card reading:

CATS

see

FELIS DOMESTICUS

Such a reference indicates that, in the specialized collection of the zoo, cats are treated scientifically and specifically. Cross-references should also be made from lay terminology to the subject access derived from a specialized thesaurus used by the library. Cross references can also create the link between the nomenclature of the museum's object collection and the library's subject headings, an important attribute for both museum staff and visitors. While "cross references make cross readers," the lack of such linkages makes for frustrated readers or inaccessible resources.

In the electronic catalog (OPAC), the cross references are usually transparent; that is, one types in CATS and up pops FELIS DOMESTICUS.

What to Catalog?

Books. The question of what items in the library's collection to include in the public catalog is not an idle one, in terms of time, money, and effort. Where there is a catalog, books seem universally to be included. In the special library particularly, the inclusion of other formats is a matter of local decision.

Serials.[7] The treatment of serials in special libraries is in marked contrast to what is standard in academic libraries.[8] A title checklist (which may be generated by the vendor) is often the method of choice, with open-shelf display of the recent issues. Or the current issue may be routed, and when returned, stored on open shelving, alphabetically by title, rather than by classification. While a complete catalog record shows the library's *holdings* of a serial title (i.e., dates, volumes, or both, on hand), many special libraries do not record holdings, usually because they do not retain backfiles for more than a year or two. When selected serials are retained, they are usually bound, or transferred to microfilm or microfiche. While readers despise microformats, their obvious advantage over bulky bound volumes is that they do not take up scarce shelf space needed for current materials.

The contents of the vertical file should also be displayed in the catalog, at least by subject, through a notation such as

CATS
Material on this subject will also be
found in the vertical file, drawer #2.

Nonprint materials. Audio and video formats that can be stored in book-like boxes and shelved with books should receive booklike cataloging treatment, even if kept in a separate shelf, cabinet, or file. (In the latter instances, location should be indicated in the catalog record.) Computer software—often in over-packaged boxes—may be treated the same way.

The location of graphics, drawings, photographs, and similar materials needs to be made known; the catalog is the most efficient way to do it. As with archives, such items are not necessarily cataloged or listed individually, but rather by group, such as "Phelps Pottery Patterns."

Databases and data sites. While software packages in boxes or on CDs may be cataloged as nonprint materials, the library will one day have to deal with off-site electronic resources on the Internet or at the end of a direct land-wire connection. Information about these resources should appear in the catalog, either as a bibliographic record, or as a note under a subject or other heading:

PETS
For other information about **PETS**, see the
URL for the American Veterinary Medicine
Association: http://www.avma.org/care4pets

An example of a bibliographic record for a title "published" on the Web may be found in the Library of Congress record for its *Weekly Subject Headings*: http://lcweb.loc.gov/catdir/cpso/wls.html

Objects. Three-dimensional items, from abacuses to zircons, present problems of storage that will be discussed under the preparation section in this chapter. The bibliographic access, however, is not a problem; information is included in the catalog, since *all* carriers of intellectual content—even teddy bears—can be described under AACR2, and their presence and location made known to the library patron.

In the course of creating bibliographic access we have also created several files.

Files

The Shelf List. The shelf list is a representation of the entire collection as it is shelved and stored in the library. For each item there is a surrogate, a primary access entry. The cards appear in the shelf list in the order in which the items appear in the collection, whether on shelves, in files, or housed elsewhere.

The shelf list is also the business record of the library. If the call number (location symbol) is added to the order card it is then used as the shelf list card, the entire history of the item is contained in one place. When an item is withdrawn from the collection, the notation to that effect is made on the shelf list card, and the card is filed in a withdrawn file, preserving the history and scope of the collection.

In the computerized library, the paper shelf list may or may not be replaced by an electronic file. While the shelf list is not a public file in the same manner as the catalog records in the OPAC, it is certainly part of the library's archives, and due the same respect. Trashing the shelf list along with the paper catalog when a retrospective conversion has been completed seems akin to tearing up the museum's handwritten charter because we now have better printing methods.

The Catalog. Once the set of records has been created for a particular item, the new material is ready for processing and the records can be filed in the catalog. (Naturally, the cards should not appear in the catalog before the item in question is ready for use.) The public catalog is usually a *dictionary catalog*; that is, one arranged alphabetically by the first significant word in the top line without regard to the meaning or function of the data. This is the simplest catalog arrangement, and the one most appropriate to small collections.

Larger collections, with extensive catalogs, sometimes find it is helpful for patrons and staff to divide the catalog according to the function of the filing line, leading to what is called a *divided catalog*. The usual arrangement in the divided catalog is to file author and title entries in one sequence and subjects in another. This strategy separates the patron with a quick look-up from the patron with the more extensive subject search.

Filing and filing rules were for long years arbitrary and idiosyncratic. In 1980, both the American Library Association and the Library of Congress published new filing rules strongly influenced by the machine logic of automated cataloging systems.[9] The ALA rules are simpler. The six main points are restated and illustrated in Appendix E. A copy of the filing principles posted conspicuously by the catalog will also assist patrons in locating access points.

Preparation, or Processing

Preparing an acquisition for use in the library collection involves a number of considerations: the nature, format, and subject of the item, its probable use and users, the library facilities and storage, and the likely shelf life of the item. The preparation procedures outlined here apply to that basic library item, the book, with suggested variations appropriate to other materials. Each library should develop a local *procedures manual* to spell out the preparation and processing decisions and to provide models of circulation cards and labels.

Books

Because books are usually the principal focus of technical services, the following discussion centers on them; most of the procedures, however, can be adapted to other media and materials, as noted at the end of this section. And whether the library is paper-based or has entered the high-tech, electronic whirl, most of the tasks of preparation are low-tech and hands-on.

Ownership. Preparation processes begin with the ownership stamp. While it is wise to refrain from stamping the materials until it is absolutely certain that the item in hand is the one ordered and that it is in acceptable condition, it is also prudent to establish ownership as soon as these determinations are made. Decide on a pattern for ownership stamps and stick to it. Most libraries stamp the top and bottom stack of pages, inside the front and back boards (covers), and some designated page (such as 32).

Order record. The order record, placed in the book after stamping, proceeds along with the book through the succeeding steps. It ultimately may either become the shelf list card, or, if a unit catalog record is used as the shelf list card, filed as a permanent record of the transaction in a file of completed orders. The book, with order card, goes then to the cataloging station, where catalog records are prepared as described before and in Appendix C.

Labels. The shelf location indicated by the label is an important aspect of preparation. The label should be clear, durable, and easily read without radical changes in the patron's posture. Experience and experimentation help determine which among the several methods of labeling materials is the most feasible. Two of the more popular labeling techniques are:

- Heat pen and transfer tape. These labels are permanent, virtually universal in application, neat and readable if prepared by someone who is painstaking and adept; but the method is slow and potentially dangerous. The pen must be preheated, so the method is better for the production of several labels at one time rather than for the occasional making of one label.

- Self-adhesive labels. Labels have varying degrees of "stickingness"; those applied with a heating iron or overlaid with a sealing strip tend to adhere longer. The call number is usually typed, a mechanical advantage over hand-lettering. Many jobbers' cataloging kits come with labels, a useful feature if the labels represent the library's decisions regarding classification.

Circulation apparatus. Jobbers' kits also come with cards and pockets—the means of preserving the record of circulation. Book (or circulation) cards and book pockets may also be purchased blank from library supply firms. The author, title, and call number must be typed on them. The pocket is glued on the front or back board, and the book card inserted in it. At the time of a circulation transaction, the borrower writes the required information on the book card, which is placed in a circulation file under the date due. The same date is stamped on a date slip affixed near the pocket.

The great drawback of the card-and-pocket system is that it may cause the library to violate a basic ethical principle of librarianship, that of *confidentiality of records*. Without exercise of other precautions, the circulation record is in plain sight, both in the file and—for a long time to come—in the book. Because the privacy rights of any citizen extend to the individual's choice of reading matter, the special librarian should be sensitive to the requirements of patron privacy.[10]

There are ways to overcome some of the deficiencies of the handy and familiar card-and-pocket system and yet preserve confidentiality: erasing the name, striking through it with black marker, taping a label over it, using the card from the bottom up, and cutting off the name when the book is returned. A higher level of privacy occurs if the patron uses a number rather than name, but the circulation record is still there later if anyone wishes to pursue the borrower's identity. It is also possible to attach a borrower slip to the permanent book card solely for the duration of the circulation period, so that when the item is returned, the link between it and the borrower is permanently broken. If the library is able to use a computerized circulation system, the link is erased at the time the item is returned. And even though circulation of materials is at first (or forever) limited to museum staff, confidentiality must not be abrogated.

Serials

Whether serials should be circulated is a policy decision of no small significance for the library's patrons, and one that needs to be consistently applied. Because serials are important for research currency, the decision should involve those most affected—the readers.

Bound volumes of serials are often treated like books; current issues are often kept within the library. However, if current issues are circulated through the loan system or routed to a list of readers, they can be temporarily placed in protective covers or binders, and treated more or less like books.

Nonprint Materials

If the library proposes an integrated collection, shelving together all the various carriers of information on the same subject, some adaptations and modifications are necessary for both storage and circulation.[11] Boxed games, videotapes, filmstrip sets, overpackaged software, CD-ROMS and audiotapes in cases rather than jackets can be treated very like books insofar as ownership, labeling, and circulation apparatus goes. Other nonbook materials may need to be repackaged: standard boxes can accommodate stray filmstrips, game pieces, and similar items. Some media, however, require specialized care or are too large, awkward, or fragile to do anything but resort to separate storage and restricted circulation. (See also chapter 4.)

The decision regarding circulation of nonbook materials (and consequently, decisions about storage as well) should be stated clearly in the library's policy manual, either as part of collection development or as a separate circulation policy. Many nonprint media require intermediary hardware. We shall discuss such requirements in chapters 4 and 7.

With the library materials selected and now organized, the library staff can turn to matters of space and equipment.

In Summary

With the desired items identified and acquired, the library staff faces the tedious but crucial task of organizing the collection for quick, easy access, and preparing the collections items for circulation.

Starting Up

1. The staff selects a classification scheme and subject heading list and learns how to use these tools.

2. The staff decides on a cataloging source and methodology,

   • creating the cataloging records in-house using available cataloging copy,

- securing catalog records from outside sources,
- using a variety of sources. (This last is the most realistic solution, but the most difficult to keep straight initially.)

In any case, the records should be in AACR2/ISBD format.

3. Supplies are purchased for cataloging and for processing the library materials.

4. The staff prepares a processing manual based on decisions in step 2. The manual will list and describe the operations sequentially, showing correctly prepared samples of all products such as labels, cards, and other items.

5. Based on the space at hand and the processing manual, the staff sets up a work-flow sequence so that various operations are performed at certain stations. With work space organized in this manner, volunteers can select and perform one operation, such as preparing book cards and pockets. All stations and all work in progress should be labeled (e.g., "Books to be shelved").

6. The staff evaluates the procedures and processes often in the beginning and makes adjustments as necessary.

Revitalizing

1. The staff evaluates the present bibliographic access, if any, and decides whether to retain it or change it. This decision should be based on future needs and programs, rather than present convenience, keeping in mind that the future may well involve an OPAC, interlibrary loan (ILL), and other telecommunication-based transactions.

2. See step 2, above.

3. See steps 3 and 4, above.

4. The staff organizes or reorganizes the work space and trains volunteers in the various operations.

5. See step 6, above.

Notes

1. Dilys E. Morris, and Gregory Wood, "Cataloging: Librarianship's Best Bargain," *Library Journal* 124/11 (15 June 1999): 44–46.

2. Karen A. Wilson, and Marylou Colver, eds., *Outsourcing Library Technical Services Operations: Practices in Academic, Public, and Special Libraries* (Chicago:

ALA, 1997); and Arnold Hirshon, and Barbara Winters, *Outsourcing Library Technical Services: A How-To-Do-It Manual for Librarians* (New York: Neal-Schuman, 1996).

3. And, for that matter, they continue to use card-based catalogs. My 1999 survey indicated that 47 percent of the respondents had card catalogs (down from 64 percent in 1994); 24 percent used some form of computerization (up from 19 percent); and 26 percent had no catalog at all. And many patrons *like* card catalogs, as witness Nicholson Baker's diatribe: "Annals of Scholarship: Discards," *The New Yorker* 70/4 (4 April 1994): 64–86; see also: Walt Crawford, "The Card Catalog and Other Digital Controversies," *American Libraries* 30/1 (January 1999): 53–58.

4. *Anglo-American Cataloguing Rules*, 2nd ed., 1988 revision (Ottawa: Canadian Library Association; Chicago: American Library Association, 1988); with amendments, 1993.

5. Arlene G. Taylor, and Rosanna M. O'Neil, *Cataloging with Copy: A Decision-Maker's Handbook,* 2nd ed. (Englewood, Col.: Libraries Unlimited, 1988.)

6. Robert G. Chenhall, *The Revised Nomenclature for Museum Cataloging: Revised and Expanded Version of Robert G. Chenhall's System for Classifying Man-Made Objects*, [by] James R. Blackaby, Patricia Greeno and the Nomenclature Committee (Walnut Creek, Calif.: AltaMira Press, 1995.)

7. For an exhaustive study of the universe of serials, albeit principally from the viewpoint of collection management in academic or large public libraries, see Thomas E. Nisonger, *Management of Serials in Libraries* (Englewood, Col.: Libraries Unlimited, 1998.)

8. In a 1997 survey, I found that only half the special libraries queried included bibliographic records for serials in the catalog, although all had catalogs, and 77 percent had online catalogs. See Esther Green Bierbaum, "Bibliographic Control of Serials in the Special Library," *Serials Librarian* 32/1-2 (1997): 163–176.

9. American Library Association, *ALA Filing Rules* (Chicago: The Association, 1980); Library of Congress, *Library of Congress Filing Rules* (Washington, D.C.: Library of Congress, 1980.)

10. K. M. Wayne, "Access and Privacy: Ethics in Library, Archival and Visual Resource Collections," *Art Documentation* 10/3 (Summer 1991): 88–89; and G. Guy Smith, "A Lawyer's Perspective on Confidentiality," *American Libraries* 19/6 (June 1988): 453.

11. For specific and detailed discussion of nonprint storage, see Jean Riddle Weihs, *The Integrated Library: Encouraging Access to Multimedia Materials*, 2nd ed. (Phoenix, Ariz.: Oryx, 1991); and the earlier edition, *Accessible Storage of Nonbook Materials* (1984).

Further Reading

Organizing the Collection

Akers, Susan Grey. *Akers' Simple Library Cataloging*. 7th ed. Edited by Arthur Curley and Jana Varlejs. Metuchen, N.J.: Scarecrow, 1984.

Buck, Rebecca A., and Jean Allman Gilmore, eds. *The New Museum Registration Methods*. 4th ed. Washington, D. C.: American Association of Museums (AAM), 1998.

Chan, Lois May. *Cataloging and Classification: An Introduction*. 2nd ed. New York: McGraw-Hill, 1994.

Downing, Mildred H., and David Downing. *Introduction to Cataloging and Classification.* 7th ed. Jefferson, N.C.: McFarland, 1992.

Hagler, Ronald. *The Bibliographic Record and Information Technology.* 3rd ed. Chicago: American Library Association (ALA); Ottawa: Canadian Library Association, 1997.

Hoffman, Herbert H. *Small Library Cataloging.* 2nd ed. Metuchen, N.J.: Scarecrow, 1986.

Intner, Sheila S., and Jean Weihs. *Special Libraries: A Cataloging Guide.* Englewood, Colorado: Libraries Unlimited, 1998.

Miller, Rosalind E., and Jane C. Terwillegar. *Commonsense Cataloging: A Cataloger's Manual.* 4th ed., rev. [of Piercy, Esther G., *Commonsense Cataloging.*] New York: H. W. Wilson, 1990.

Palmer, Joseph W. *Cataloging and the Small Special Library.* Washington, D.C.: Special Libraries Association, 1992.

Reibel, Daniel B. *Registration Methods for Small History Museums: A Guide for Historical Collections.* 2nd ed., rev. Yardley, Pennsylvania: DBR Publications, 1991.

_____. *Registration Methods for the Small Museum.* 3rd ed. Walnut Creek, Calif.: AltaMira Press, 1997.

Taylor, Arlene G. *The Organization of Information.* Englewood, Colorado: Libraries Unlimited, 1999.

_____, and Rosanna M. O'Neil. *Cataloging with Copy: A Decision-Maker's Handbook.* 2nd ed. Littleton, Col.: Libraries Unlimited, 1988.

Wynar, Bohdan. *Introduction to Cataloging and Classification.* 9th ed., by Arlene G. Taylor. Englewood, Col.: Libraries Unlimited, 2000.

Description

Baker, Nicholson. "Annals of Scholarship: Discards." *The New Yorker* 70/4 (4 April 1994): 64–86.

Gorman, Michael. *The Concise AACR2.* 1988 revision. Chicago: ALA, 1988.

Cf. Reibel, *supra,* and Paul W. Winkler, eds., for the Joint Steering Committee. *Anglo-American Cataloguing Rules.* 2nd ed., 1988 Revision. Chicago: ALA, 1988; with amendments, 1993.

Maxwell, Robert L., and Margaret F. Maxwell. *Maxwell's Handbook for AACR2R: Explaining and Illustrating the Anglo-American Cataloguing Rules and the 1993 Amendments.* Chicago: ALA, 1997.

Classification

Chan, Lois Mai, John P. Comaromi, Joan S. Mitchell, and Mohinder P. Satija. *Dewey Decimal Classification: A Practical Guide.* 2nd ed., revised for DDC 21. Albany, N.Y.: OCLC/Forest Press, 1996.

Dewey, Melvil. *Abridged Dewey Decimal Classification.* 13th ed. Albany, N.Y.: Forest Press/OCLC, 1997.

_____. *Dewey Decimal Classification and Relative Index.* Edition 21. Edited by Joan S. Mitchell *et al.* Albany, N.Y.: Forest Press/OCLC, 1996. 4 vols.

Dewey Decimal Classification: Additions, Notes and Decisions (DC&.) Albany, N.Y.: Forest Press/OCLC, now only available at http://www.oclc.org/fp/ (accessed August 2000).

Hunter, Eric J. *Classification Made Simple*. Brookfield, Vt.: Gower, 1988.
Library of Congress, Subject Cataloging Division. *Library of Congress Classification: Classes A–Z*. Various editions. Washington, D.C.: The Library, 1896– . 40+ vols.

Subject Access

Chenhall, Robert G. *The Revised Nomenclature for Museum Cataloging: A Revised and Expanded Version of Robert G. Chenhall's System for Classifying Man-made Objects*, [by] James R. Blackaby, Patricia Greeno, and the Nomenclature Committee. Walnut Creek, Calif.: AltaMira Press, 1995.
Lancaster, F. Wilfrid. *Vocabulary Control for Information Retrieval*. Arlington, Va.: Information Resources Press, 1986.
Library of Congress, Subject Cataloging Division. *Library of Congress Subject Headings*. 23rd ed. Washington, D.C.: The Library, 2000. 5 vols. Annual. (Also n microfiche and on CD-ROM and datatape.)
Library of Congress. *Library of Congress Subject Headings Weekly List*. Washington, D.C.: Cataloging Policy and Support Office, available at: http://lcweb.loc.gov/catdir/cpso/wls.html (accessed August 2000).
Sears, Minnie Earl. *Sears List of Subject Headings*. 15th ed. Edited by Martha T. Mooney. New York: H.W. Wilson, 1994.

Technical Services and Processing

American Library Association. *ALA Filing Rules*. Chicago: ALA, 1980.
Crawford, Walt. *MARC for Library Use: Understanding Integrated USMARC*. 2nd edition. Boston: G.K. Hall, 1989.
Dunn, Walter S. "Cataloging Ephemera: A Procedure for Small Libraries." Nashville, Tenn.: AASLH, 1972. (Technical Leaflet no. 58.)
Evans, G. Edward, and Sandra M. Heft. *Introduction to Technical Services*. 6th ed. Englewood, Col.: Libraries Unlimited, 1994.
Hahn, Harvey. "Technical Services in the Small Library." Chicago: ALA/LAMA, 1987. (Library Administration and Management Association Small Libraries Publications.)
Hirshon, Arnold. *Outsourcing Library Technical Services: A How-To-Do-It Manual for Librarians*. New York: Neal-Schuman, 1996.
Library of Congress. *Library of Congress Filing Rules*. Washington, D.C.: The Library, 1980.
Nisonger, Thomas E. *Management of Serials in Libraries*. Englewood, Col.: Libraries Unlimited, 1998.
Wayne, K. M. "Access and Privacy: Ethics in Library, Archival and Visual Resource Collections." *Art Documentation* 10 (Summer 1991): 88–89.
Weihs, Jean Riddle. *The Integrated Library: Encouraging Access to Multimedia Materials*. 2nd ed. Phoenix, Ariz.: Oryx, 1991. (Rev. ed. of *Accessible Storage of Nonbook Materials*, 1984.)
Wilson, Karen A., and Marylou Colver, eds. *Outsourcing Library Technical Services Operations: Practices in Academic, Public, and Special Libraries*. Chicago: ALA, 1997.

Chapter 4

Nuts and Bolts:
Space, Furnishings,
Equipment, and Security

When it comes to space and facilities for museum library and information services, it is easy to make a list of *desiderata*:

1. A *central location*, easily accessible to the library's patrons—whether staff, public, or both—and made known by directional signs throughout the building and a listing on the building directory;

2. A single, attractive, welcoming *entrance*, inviting and clearly marked;

3. An interior *climate* controlled for the comfort of staff and patrons and for the safety and security of the materials;

4. Glareless, unshadowed, natural and artificial *lighting*, which is both adequate and unobtrusive;

5. A spacious, attractive, lively *interior*, efficiently ordered to provide space and good traffic flow for:

   • Shelving and storage sufficient for double the present collection;

   • Reading and study tables and carrels;

   • A lounge area with magazine display;

   • A reader services desk (not counter);

- A prominent, accessible location for the catalog, whether card drawers or OPAC;

- A display and exhibit area;

6. An *office area* for the librarian;

7. A *workroom* with cabinets, counter and storage space, and running water
   for various processing activities;

8. *Electric and telecommunication wiring* to meet the present and future
   needs for voice, video, media, and computers—that is, an adequate number of unshared lines and handily located outlets,[1] which are *not* seques-
   tered behind shelves or placed beyond normal reach; telephone lines for
   both voice and computer communication; and coaxial, fiber, and other
   cabling as may be needed.

Planning help can be found in the library as well as the architectural literature. During the golden age of library construction in the 1960s and 1970s, a
flood of titles on library planning and building appeared, but now it has subsided
to a trickle. Since the principles of space and construction do not change, much
of the literature remains useful, with a caveat: the librarian must be aware that
many of today's requirements for equipment and services were unheard of twenty
years ago.[2] Whether the space is to be new or recycled, the key to efficient facilities is careful planning, including visits to other museum libraries.[3]

In his article "Museum Library Facilities," M. Noël Balke makes useful distinctions among the desirable features listed above, categorizing them in terms
of "premises, fixtures and furniture,"[4] or the physical space, the utilities, and what
goes in the space. We shall consider space and utilities together and then discuss furniture and equipment. In actual planning, of course, space, furniture and
equipment fit together like the pieces of a puzzle—and are sometimes just about
as amenable to solution as an all-one-color jigsaw. So, while we speak of them
separately for the sake of convenience, decisions about one ripple an influence
over the others. If the planning for the various aspects is being handled by
different committees, the Furnishings Committee needs to communicate with the
Equipment Committee, and both must consult with the Space Committee!

Space

First Considerations

The initial considerations in determining space needs are, of course, the
library's goals, for they will strongly influence the amount of space needed and

what goes on in it. For example, the library that plans to serve museum administration and staff only has different space requirements from those of the library that plans also to serve members or the public as well. On the other hand, if the library initially focuses on space needs for staff and administration while thinking vaguely of including members in the future, then the space that is sufficient now will be outgrown in the future.

In most museums, space is a precious commodity; it is doled out, not claimed. Even if the space allotted for information services has few or none of the features in the list above, library planning can continue. Museum libraries have grown from cloakrooms to buildings of their own. With adaptations of use, storage, and services, a single redeeming feature can be enhanced. A cloakroom, for example, may have the real estate criterion of location to recommend it; it is often centrally located and accessible. The librarian faced with that challenge may locate the catalog and information services in the cloakroom and disperse the collections to classrooms and staff areas—not an ideal situation, but far better than giving up before beginning.

Space Needs

Space needs also depend upon proposed services, which in turn are derived from the museum's mission and the library's goals. For example, if members use the library only upon appointment, there is less need for study space than if the members are welcomed to come in whenever the museum is open, thereby creating traffic jams at opening and closing hours and child pick-up times.

Older, but still-valid, standards for square footage, shelving, and other physical features may be found in the Special Libraries Association's "Objectives and Standards for Special Libraries."[5] Balke and Mount also provide schematics and tables of space requirements for different types of furniture and equipment.[6] Vendors of library furnishings and equipment often provide planning assistance.

A scale floor plan—or better yet, a scale model of the library space—helps the library planner visualize the position of shelving and other furniture to avoid such potential trouble spots as oddly-placed windows and air vents scheduled to be located behind shelving. For the technically oriented planners, CAD (computer-assisted design) software is both fun and helpful.

Nonbook and nonprint materials require special spaces, even if the library as far as possible pursues an integrated collection.[7] Audiovisual media, which are neither audible nor visible without intermediating hardware, either must be shelved near the hardware or special provision must be made to bring media and intermedia together—with signs directing patrons to the collection, or through an informational note in the catalog.

A note about rehabilitated quarters. Second floors, particularly in historic houses and buildings, may require bracing or even replacing before bearing the load of a library collection. Hence, beware the second floor. Books and journals are dead weight and are far heavier than might at first appear (approximately 25 pounds per cubic foot). An engineer should evaluate the load-bearing capabilities of joists, stringers, and flooring in any old building and should be consulted in planning library space in a new building.

A number of other considerations enter into space planning and use.

Security. Security is a primary spatial concern. Certain materials, by their condition, rarity, importance, or fragility are unsuitable for general shelving. The list of such materials is different for each library and so is the storage solution. If these materials are stored in a locked drawer or cabinet, the catalog information on them should include use restrictions. This type of security is found in any library, including those open only to museum staff.[8]

For the museum library that is open to the public, the first and best defense for the collection is a single entrance with an information services desk or table located nearby. The most effective defensive strategy, however, is to keep keys in pockets or drawers, and out of sight.[9] Bookmarks, posters, and policies can offer gentle reminders regarding care and respect for library materials; as Chadwick notes, such reminders, unhappily, apply also to staff.[10] Unfortunately, whether willfully or inadvertently, human beings remain the greatest threat to the collection.[11]

Security for computers in public areas has increasingly become a matter of concern. The machines themselves and connected printers can be locked to their tables. Locking devices are also available for CD-ROM drives (if not integrated into the computer) and video and audio players. To protect the integrity of the bibliographic databases, when the OPAC is not cabled to a server elsewhere, it should offer catalog functions only; general use computers can be located separately from the OPAC. When the library circulates software, it is a good general policy to keep nothing on the hard drive but the operating system, in order to protect the licensing agreement.

The library that offers online service and Internet access opens a fascinating and richly varied world to its patrons, along with a whole new set of security issues for the institution. Filtering devices and First Amendment rights are hotly debated issues in the library press. The wisest course is to keep up with the literature and to seek guidance from the museum's legal counsel.

The library must also conform to the overall museum security measures for theft and damage caused by humans and for fire and storm emergencies. To that end, the staff must devise a disaster plan—although no one wishes to contemplate needing one. Such a plan, first, "will secure the collections against the threat of disaster and, secondly, provides adequate support facilities should disaster strike."[12]

This means that policies are established for library materials under these circumstances of duress. For example, in order to preserve water-damaged books, the librarian should arrange to use a freezer locker in advance; after the pipe breaks is too late. When particularly valuable materials are at risk, the librarian may wish to consult a security service and local fire control units for information about fire security and chemical suppressants. For libraries, the effects of water are often more to be feared than those of fire.

The library's collections are also an aspect of the museum's overall risk management program. Should calamity occur, an accurate and current inventory and a valuation for major individual items as well as a total assessment are necessary for an insurance claim.

Climate Control. While human comfort is certainly a consideration, heating and air conditioning are also aspects of security in that a controlled climate preserves the materials from nonhuman abuse. Air handling systems should control dirt, mildew, and insects and other biota as well as temperature and humidity.

Air handling systems can not do it alone; cleanliness has as much to do with safe-guarding materials as it does with godliness. For this reason, carpeting and upholstery come under scrutiny—carpeting for the added reason of static induction around computers.[13]

Lighting. Light must also be considered with space. Natural, filtered daylight is the most pleasant and comfortable lighting for library patrons. Artificial light that most nearly mimics daylight is usually considered ideal. What is ideal for people, however, is not necessarily ideal for library materials. The library planner should take into account the deleterious effects of light upon bindings and paper, so that the type of lighting installed is appropriate to the materials and the area of the library. If suspended fixtures are used, be sure to know before installation begins which way the shelving will run so that the fixtures are not hung crosswise to the shelves, a situation that casts shadows on half of the books.

Audiovisual equipment is but one type of hardware the library must consider. Furniture is needed to take care of equipment; so we shall consider it first, although everything comes tumbling in at once when the library is getting started.

Furniture

Even though the characteristics of the physical space influence everything else about the library facilities, furniture selection is the psychological starting point. The kind and amount of furniture selected is subject to fiscal resources, space allotments, and library goals.

Even if the museum library is confined initially to such functions as collection development and preparation and to such services as staff borrowing and reference service, a certain amount and type of furniture is necessary. In preparing the list of furniture and equipment needed, it may be possible to earmark some pieces as candidates for memorial gifts. Four types of furnishings are essential: shelving and storage, tables and desks, seating, and the catalog case or the accommodations for the OPAC.

Shelving. Whether called book shelving, book storage, or stacks, the furniture on which books are stored requires a considerable outlay of funds, as a glance at a library supply catalog will confirm. It is often possible to find locally constructed shelving at less cost. The product should, however, have standard dimensions and include such details of construction as adjustable shelves, kickplates, and connectors. Inexpensive shelving has drawbacks: if it is made of wood, the sections tend to warp and sag; if it is metal, shelves sag and, worse, iron oxide transfers to library materials and library patrons.

Library planners often underestimate shelving needs. The rule-of-thumb volume count of about 200 books to a single-faced standard shelving section sounds generous, but the librarian needs to remember that shelves should remain no more than two-thirds to three-fourths full (the so-called working capacity). Even when the library planner purchases enough shelves for them to remain only half-full or plans for twice the running footage estimated for the first five years, the shelves almost immediately fill to capacity.

Special shelving needs also must be considered. Will there be a separate reference section, with waist-high shelves and a nearby table? Will there be a magazine display, in addition to shelving for bound volumes and for backfiles stored in binders or flat on the shelves? Will audiovisual materials be stored separately but accessibly, in boxes on shelves, in files or bins? What about compact discs? Videos? Three-dimensional objects? Even though the library has not yet purchased the first CD or geology model, the earliest planning stages are not too soon to think about how and where such materials will be stored.

In all instances of planning materials storage, patron use and comfort are primary considerations. For example, the free-standing revolving kiosks for video display require both standing and stooping room.

When, as in the case of the revitalized library, a larger collection is on hand and is expected to expand, consideration should be given to compact shelving, which frees up floor space for other uses while also accommodating more volumes.[14] The Seattle Museum of Art, for example, has been able to accommodate some 15,000 books and other bound volumes on its compact shelves, thus leaving room in a relatively small space for amenities such as comfortable seating.

As stated earlier, the librarian cannot overlook the calculation of flooring deadload capabilities in deliberations about what kind of shelving and storage to buy.[15]

An exhibit area or display case is a popular and lively addition to the museum library furnishings. It can be used to highlight library materials, to advertise museum programs, to tie the library to the work of curators and exhibitors through exhibited documents and library materials, or to arouse public curiosity with teaser presentations of objects or books.

Tables and Desks. Librarians are coming out from behind their former bunker-inspired three-sided counters, those physical and psychological barriers that tended to keep patrons at bay, if not cowed. Particularly in the special library, where circulation procedures take up less time and room than in public or academic libraries, the patron service desk is often table height and more table-like, distinguished from other tables, perhaps, by a sign demanding, "Please interrupt!" Even when circulation is a large consideration (in the museum library serving children, for example), check-out procedures can be conducted from a standard desk or table.

To begin with, then, the tables ordered for patron use can also be used for the librarian's station. Long tables are not greatly favored by Americans. (Observe library readers at long tables and you will see that, when there is space to spread out, readers will locate themselves along the long sides, calculatedly facing across at an empty chair.) Patrons favor instead shorter tables (four or five feet in length rather than six or eight), round tables, and individual carrels. Modular pieces that can be arranged in various configurations are also good selections.

If computers are provided for patrons, clusters of carrels offer patron privacy and also convenience for the librarian. The computer dedicated as an OPAC can be placed for reader convenience.

Tables fitted with shelves atop one long side and designed for using indexes and ready reference materials are nice to have, but the library can use other options, such as placing low shelves nearby, so that the most necessary furniture is purchased first.

Floor space, of course, determines the number of tables. Tables do not have to be lumped together; attractive and inviting spaces can be created by placing tables in the shelving area. If children use study areas, provide at least one child-size table and scaled-down seating.

As in the case of shelving, quality of product is a primary consideration; however, institutional-grade furniture no longer needs to *look* institutional. Hence, nonfunctional, decorative pieces (such as parson's tables, the legs of which pull off with the first push) and decorator finishes (which normal library use quickly renders beyond restoration) are not necessary for attractive appearances.

Seating. Quality and sturdiness of construction are also important in chair selection. A full complement of seating should be provided for each table, regardless of American seating patterns, including in-scale seating for junior patrons.

Study table seating is rather standard. For the computer carrels, however, swivel desk chairs may prove popular. And if there is a magazine display, or even just a corner near a window with a low table, a grouping of upholstered pieces creates a visually attractive area. Beanbag floor cushions are the seating of choice for the younger readers.

Catalog. Unless the library is already served by a computer-based catalog—or plans one in the immediate future—a card catalog case is a necessary piece of furniture. The number of drawers will be dictated by the number of items anticipated for the collection, keeping in mind that each item will require an average of five or six bibliographic records to provide an array of access points. Plan to fill drawers no more than two-thirds full. Library supply catalogs usually state the drawer capacity in number of cards; find out what proportion of the drawer that number represents. It is better to have excess capacity in the beginning than to be crowded in the near future.

Again, quality of product is an essential consideration; library catalogs receive hard use over time, and there is nothing quite as dismaying as a drawer front that separates from its drawer. Librarians now have a wide choice of styles and finishes in catalog cases, so that the catalog can match or contrast with the rest of the furnishings. Card retainer rods, drawer stops, easy-to-use pull hardware, and drawer-front labels are requisites, no matter the style or size.

If start-up funds simply cannot be stretched to cover a library catalog case, the library may use a bank of 3 × 5–inch card-file drawers temporarily—very temporarily in the case of metal drawers. There are several inherent dangers in using such files, however. First, there is the constant possibility of having the contents of a drawer inadvertently dumped, with unhappy results to the alphabetical arrangement. Second, patrons can remove a bibliographic record from the file too easily. Third, the drawers were not meant for constant use and can result in rust stains, smashed fingers, and distracting noise. The cost-benefit of a standard catalog case should be reconsidered in comparison with the problems introduced by metal—or even wooden—card-file drawers. Since the shelf list, order file, and probably the serials records are not normally public files (although museum staff certainly should not be barred from consulting them), it is possible to use ordinary card file drawers for these records.

The card catalog is often listed as equipment, but since it is prominently situated in the public area of the library and should be as attractive to the eye as the other pieces there, we have included it in the discussion of furnishings. The range of other equipment available is amazing and constantly growing. The following section will list and discuss some of the items which museum librarians have found to be useful and effective.

Equipment

Equipment can range from high to low technology. More possibilities will be discussed when looking at technology in chapter 8. What we turn to now are the items that will make opening day possible.

Vertical Files. Also called letter files, these banks of drawers are an essential item for the storage of library business documents, as well as clippings, and other materials and ephemera that are documentary data sources. If the nonbook, nonserial collections stored in vertical files are not open to the public and consequently are stored out of sight in the workroom, the appearance of the files will not be of as great concern as the looks of vertical files in the public areas.

If shelved materials are accessible to library patrons, and if the headings for the vertical file materials are noted in the card catalog or OPAC, then vertical file materials should also be accessible to researchers and readers, and their storage cases should be similar in style to the others in the public area.

Files come in two sizes, letter and legal, which accommodate 8½ × 11–inch and 8½ × 14–inch materials, respectively. If the library anticipates heavy use of the vertical files, it is better, considering the slight difference in cost between the two sizes, to start with legal-size files, since they can accommodate most documents in unfolded condition as well as graphic materials and other oversized sheets of paper.

Librarians have a tendency to overstuff vertical files. One control strategy is to fit the drawers with frames that allow folders to be hung, rather than jammed, in the drawer. A second strategy is to use sidewise sliding drawers, which, when pulled out, make the entire depths of the drawers accessible, whereas in front-to-back sliding drawers, the rear three or four inches elude all but the most determined and athletic searchers.

Typewriter. A typewriter—however old-fashioned it may seem in the glow of the computer screen—is a handy piece of equipment to have around for memos, labels, and (in the paper environment) catalog cards. But even an electronic typewriter makes a certain amount of noise, and for that reason, and also because typewriters are regarded as low-tech and clerical, this essential equipment is best located in the workroom or office.

Computers. In contrary strategy, the relatively hi-tech computer may be located in the public area, either near the information service desk, or, if the staff will be using it to assist patrons with database searches, in the carrel or table seating area. While the keyboard does click, the noise output seems minor compared to that of a typewriter. A noisy printer, however, should be banished to the workroom or fitted with a muffling hood. (More on computers in chapter 8.)

Audiovisual Equipment. If the collection includes sound or visual recordings, the library needs the equipment necessary to make them audible or visible. Thus the decision to collect a nonprint format implies as well the decision to acquire the hardware and store it somewhere in the museum. In some museums, the education department is responsible for the hardware, while the library stores and controls the media; this division works well where the education department is the exclusive user of the media and where the collection is not open to patrons other than museum staff.

When museum members are also library users, their access to media may be limited to on-site use, in which case the library must be able to provide the equipment and a viewing or listening spot. Earphones and an audiovisual carrel will usually suffice for such on-site use. If off-site borrowing is permitted, then decisions must be made *and posted* regarding the availability of equipment.

Librarians may generally assume that borrowers own or can obtain carousel slide projectors, video cassette and compact disc players, and audiotape cassette players. "Movie" (16-mm film) projectors, filmstrip projectors, record players, DVD and compact disc computer devices, and overhead projectors are less likely to be owned by the average family; single-concept (8-mm cartridge) film projectors, 2 × 2–inch (glass) slide projectors, and microscopes, not at all.

Each audiovisual transaction should be accompanied by care instructions both for the media and for the equipment. Some libraries require a deposit against the return of the equipment and to cover the spare lamps, which should be provided with the equipment.

Whether or not equipment use is confined to in-house hearing or viewing, the library should purchase *institutional-grade* equipment if possible. The slight difference in cost will be made up in trouble-free usage. The availability of local service is a factor also. It is often possible to arrange a blanket service contract with a local audiovisual service, a way to ensure that routine maintenance is performed to ward off large repair charges.

The management of audiovisual collections is a broad and specialized area within librarianship. The museum librarian who anticipates an extensive collection in terms of numbers or circulated use should consult a book devoted to the topic.

Circulation Equipment. Whatever circulation system the library decides to use, it will require some paraphernalia such as stamps, cards and files, and so on. Whether there is a circulation station or the information service desk takes care of all patron needs, the equipment should ideally be self-contained, in a box that can be placed in a desk drawer. If circulation procedures are handled on a self-service basis for museum staff, a sign clearly explaining the procedures needs to be added to the equipment.

Tool Kit. Along with the first piece of library furniture or equipment, the librarian should acquire a small tool kit. Especially handy is the tool with one handle and interchangeable fittings that include various sizes of screwdrivers, including the finest jeweler's and the two standard sizes of Phillips screwdrivers. Also necessary are pliers (one needle-nosed), a small adjustable wrench, a steel tape measure, and a tap hammer. The tool kit should be stored in a safe place— one known only to library staff.

Supplies Kit. The ready-assembled kits of office supplies are handily self-contained and portable. Moreover, there is only one purchase order involved. The equivalent in scissors, tape, paper clips, glue stick, markers, and adhesive notes, together with a suitable container, can also be purchased in one trip to an office supply store.

Materials Preparation Kit. While more likely to be classified as supplies than equipment, the labels, cards, and stamps used in preparing materials for circulation can also be assembled in a portable, self-contained kit, easily used by a volunteer working at a service site or work place. For example, volunteers who staff the museum information desk may also be trained to prepare library materials and can often handle both tasks at once. (Other preparation equipment will be discussed in chapter 6.)

The foregoing furniture and equipment items should see the library through opening day. Browsing through the catalogs published by library supply houses will give the librarian more ideas than the budget can hold. The librarian needs to keep in mind that both furniture and equipment should be of sound construction, simple to use, essential to the efficiency of the library's operations as determined by its goals and objectives, and—where possible—attractively designed, comfortable, and user-oriented.

In Summary

Bearing in mind that for many patrons *library* is indistinguishable from *place*, staff should set about making the most of library space, arranging furniture and equipment in ways that invite patrons to linger, ensure convenient access to materials, and allow for personal safety and collection safeguarding.

Starting Up

1. The librarian and staff or committee meet with the museum administration and its board or building committee to select a *library location*. It may be necessary initially to settle for a cramped space if it is strategically located, although with the understanding that such a location is a temporary compromise. Planners must be mindful also of long-range goals of the library and its ultimately intended patrons. The librarian

should remember that space is not only valued by the square foot but is also symbolic of turf, power, importance, and other political and personal issues not necessarily invoked during planning discussions and space negotiations.

2. The library staff determines *furniture needs* in keeping with space and proposed services. Furnishings will likely need to be listed and acquired in order of importance. Substantial pieces, such as catalog case, desks, stacks, are candidates for memorial or other special gifts.

3. In the same way, and at the same time, *equipment needs* are determined, assessed, and listed. Again, planning must accommodate both present status and future growth.

Revitalizing

1. The *present library space* should be assessed in terms of location, size, wiring, and so on. If the location is good but the space will be inadequate, the library staff and committee can negotiate for more space—taking in a nearby room, perhaps—or consider decentralizing some functions and services. Previous comments about turf also apply.

2. The present *furniture* must also be evaluated, whether for discard (or trade with another department), temporary retention, or permanent retention. Decisions and projections regarding the collection size and type, card and computerized catalogs, and potential patrons (and, therefore, circulation, seating, and shelving) will influence furniture replacement and purchases.

3. The library probably already has certain items of *equipment*, some of which will need to be replaced, and some of which will need augmenting.

Notes

1. Ruth A. Fraley and Carol Lee Anderson, *Library Space Planning* (New York: Neal-Schuman, 1985), pp. 50–52.

2. For some current general guidance on facilities planning, see Ellis Mount and Renée Massoud, *Special Libraries and Information Centers: An Introductory Text,* 4th ed. (Washington, D.C.: Special Libraries Association, 1999), pp. 231–246.

3. Ellis Mount, ed., *Creative Planning of Special Library Facilities* (New York: Haworth, 1988), pp. 3–27; 41–52.

4. M. Noël Balke, "Museum Library Facilities," in John C. Larsen, ed., *Museum Librarianship*, pp. 115–130 (Hamden, Conn.: Library Professional Publications, 1985).

5. Special Libraries Association, "Objectives and Standards for Special Libraries," *Special Libraries* 55/10 (December 1964): 671–680.

6. Balke, "Museum Library Facilities," pp. 118–123; Mount, *Creative Planning*, pp. 81–98.

7. Jean Riddle Weihs, *The Integrated Library: Encouraging Access to Multimedia Materials*, 2nd ed. (Phoenix, Ariz.: Oryx, 1991).

8. New standards and specific procedures for archival and rare materials are found in draft form in "Guidelines for the Security of Rare Book, Manuscript, and Other Special Collections: A Draft," *College & Research Libraries News* 50/4 (April 1999): 304–311. Available at: http://www.ala.org/acrl/guides/index.html (updated 15 June 2000; accessed August 2000).

9. Michael Lineberry, formerly a sergeant in the Washington State University security department and now a security consultant, notes that the theft of rare books is often abetted because the keys to the secure area are left dangling on a handy nail. See Michael Lineberry, "Stop in the Name of the Law!" presentation at the Special Libraries Association conference (78 : 1992), San Francisco (audiotape).

10. William E. Chadwick, "Special Collections and Library Security: An Internal Audit Perspective," *Journal of Library Administration* 25/1 (1998): 15–31.

11. Graeme Gardiner, "Disaster Planning and Preparation: Some Basic Concepts," *Museum International*, No. 192, 48/4 (1996): 40–44.

12. Gardiner, "Disaster Planning," p. 40.

13. Jeannette Woodward, "Countdown to a New Library: Blueprint for Success," *American Libraries* 30/4 (April 1999): 44–47.

14. Bruce J. MacFadden *et al.*, "Compactors in Small Collection-Based Museum Libraries," *Curator* 31/2 (1988): 137–140.

15. See MacFadden, "Compactors," p. 138. Their three-rail system of six shelving sections was calculated to weigh nearly a ton and a half, loaded.

Further Reading

Space and Design

ARLIS/NA (Art Libraries Association of North America). *Facilities Standards for Art Libraries and Visual Resources Collections.* Edited by Betty Jo Irvine. Englewood, Col.: Libraries Unlimited, 1991.

Balke, M. Noël. "Museum Library Facilities." In John C. Larsen, ed. *Museum Librarianship*, pp. 115–130. Hamden, Conn.: Library Professional Publications, 1985.

Boss, Richard W. *Information Technologies and Space Planning for Libraries and Information Centers.* Boston: G.K. Hall, 1987.

Brooks, James, and James Draper. *Interior Design for Libraries.* Chicago: ALA, 1979.

Dahlgren, Anders. *Planning the Small Public Library Building.* Chicago: ALA/LAMA (Library Administration and Management Association), 1985.

Fraley, Ruth A., and Carol Lee Anderson. *Library Space Planning: How to Assess, Allocate, and Reorganize Collections, Resources, and Physical Facilities.* New York: Neal-Schuman, 1985.

Freifeld, Roberta, and Caryl Masyr. *Space Planning.* Washington, D.C.: Special Libraries Association (SLA), 1991.

George, Gerald, and Cindy Sherrell-Leo. *Starting Right: A Basic Guide to Museum Plan-ning*. Nashville, Tenn.: American Association of State and Local History (AASLH), 1986.

Kirby, John. *Creating the Library Identity: A Manual of Design*. Aldershot, Hants (Eng-land); Brookfield, Vt.: Gower, 1985.

Mount, Ellis, ed. *Creative Planning of Special Library Facilities.* New York: Haworth, 1988.

Rovelstad, Howard. "Guidelines for Planning Facilities for Sci-Tech Libraries." *Science and Technology Libraries* 3/4(Summer 1983): 3–19.

Smith, Beryl K., ed. *Space Planning for the Art Library*. Tucson, Ariz.: ARLIS/NA, 1991.

Stephens, Suzanne, ed. *Building the New Museum*. New York: Architectural League, 1986.

Security

Buchanan, Sally. *Disaster Planning: Preparedness and Recovery for Libraries and Archives*. Paris: General Information Programmes and UNISIST, 1988.

Clark, Edward F. "Law Enforcement and the Library." *Journal of Library Administra-tion* 25/1 (May/June 1998): 33–48.

Fennelly, Lawrence J. *Museum, Archive, and Library Security*. Boston: Butterworths, 1983.

Florian, Mary-Lou E. *Heritage Eaters: Insects and Fungi in Heritage Collections.* Lon-don: James & James, 1997.

Fortson, Judith. *Disaster Planning and Recovery: A How-to-Do-It Manual for Librari-ans and Archivists*. New York: Neal-Schuman, 1992.

Gardiner, Graeme. "Disaster Planning and Preparation: Some Basic Concepts." *Museum International*, No. 192, 48/4 (1996): 40–44.

Huntsberry, J. Stephen. "Stop in the Name of the Law!" Special Libraries Association Conference (78 : 1992), San Francisco. Audiotape.

Trinkley, Michael. *Hurricane! Surviving the Big One: A Primer for Libraries, Museums, and Archives*. 2nd ed. Columbia, S.C.: Chicora Foundation; Atlanta, Ga.: Southeast-ern Library Network, 1998.

Trinkus-Randall, Gregor. "Library and Archival Security: Policies and Procedures to Protect Holdings from Theft and Damage." *Journal of Library Administration* 25/1 (May/June 1998): 91–113.

Upton, Murray S. *Disaster Planning and Emergency Treatments in Museums*. Canberra (Australia): Institute for the Conservation of Cultural Material, 1978.

Furnishings and Storage

Pierce, William S. *Furnishing the Library Interior*. New York: Marcel Dekker, 1980.

Weihs, Jean Riddle. *Accessible Storage of Nonbook Materials*. Phoenix, Ariz.: Oryx, 1984. See also the 2nd ed.: *The Integrated Library*, 1991.

Woodward, Jeannette. "Countdown to a New Library: A Blueprint for Success." *Amer-ican Libraries* 30/4 (April 1999): 44–46.

Chapter 5

Administration: People, Planning, Budgets, and Marketing

In the preceding chapter, we discussed the ways of meeting space and equipment requirements in the museum library. In this chapter we first consider the place of the library within the museum's administrative and staff structure. Then we look at people and their requirements, at the plans they undertake, the resources they need to execute the plans, and the ways they convey their plans to others.

The Organizational Setting

As noted in chapter 1, the support of the museum's board and administration is essential to the success of the library, whether starting-up or revitalizing. Recent research indicates that the value of the library and librarian in the eyes of museum directors has increased in the last fifteen or so years. In the early 80s, not only did administrators express negative feelings toward the library, but many failed even to acknowledge their library's existence.[1] Since then, both the administrators' opinion of the library and the librarians' opinion of the administrator's use of the library have risen, if not to stratospheric heights, at least to a level that holds promise for the future role of library and information services in the museum.

Something else has been happening: In the corporate and not-for-profit worlds, new organizational models are replacing the old, top-down, strict hierarchies—the "big bugs have bigger bugs that jump on 'em and bite 'em" layers of management, as traditionally diagrammed in fig.5.1 and 5.2.

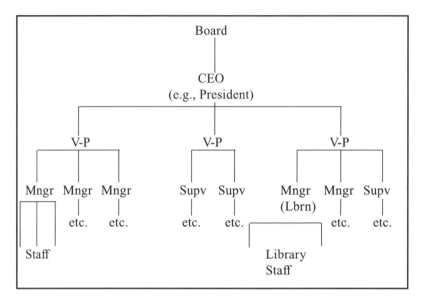

Figure 5.1: Typical hierarchical organizational structure.

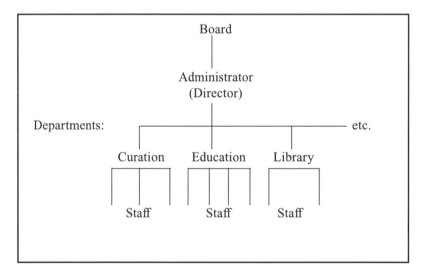

Figure 5.2: The flatter hierarchical organizational structure usually found in museums, with department heads reporting to the director.

In creative and successful organizations, the mechanical, direct-drive is giving way to an organic structure of self-organizing entities, in which the essential value is information, or knowledge.[2] These entities, variously called task forces, teams, or groups, are not static, but change members, alliances, and goals as circumstances change inside and outside the organization. Where the organization itself becomes a set of groups and teams, the staff members find they must reorient their organizational concept from top-down to interrelated-interconnected.[3]

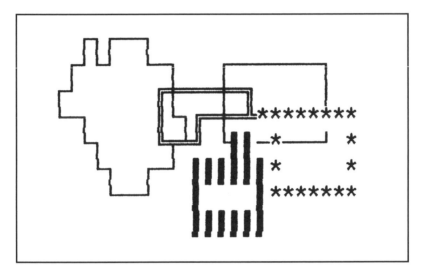

Figure 5.3: The Organic Model of Organization. Groups of varying size and configuration interact directly or indirectly with one another and with the library (=).

These changes from hierarchical to organic structures have often been as disconcerting as the disappearance of middle management that resulted from corporate weight-loss programs, where much of the new leanness has been achieved at the expense of the middle management beltline, making that a less attractive position. Libraries and information centers in corporations have been affected in varying degrees; adapting to new structures was one of the challenges of the late 1990s.

Even though the new terminology may not be familiar to the successful, mission-focused museum, where knowledge-based, interdependent enterprises (otherwise known as registration, education, preservation, and so on) have been known and accepted, the organic model is a known condition. Hence the museum library, as an entity within the larger organization and serving the information needs of all the other enterprises and departments, stands to gain the most from an interrelated structure.

But people, planning, and resources are still necessary to secure a place at the organization's table, whether the museum is structured organically, hierarchically, or somewhere in between.

Library Staff

Management consists of the planning, oversight, activities, functions, and processes that meld people, plans, and resources into an organic, unified, and purposeful organization. This means that even in the most free-wheeling, entrepreneurial organization, someone assumes ultimate responsibility for what happens. In other words, somewhere, someone is in charge. In the museum library that person is, ideally, a professional librarian.

The reality, however, is that in over half of our museums the title is vested in someone who is a willing advocate, but not an information professional.[4] That being the case, the librarian and library staff should seek professional advice and use available books and resources to gain the knowledge necessary to operate the library efficiently and effectively.

The Librarian

The essential criteria for any profession are a vocation or calling, advanced training in a body of knowledge, and the practice of intellectual skills in the service of others. For librarians, these criteria translate into a commitment to all types of carriers of intellectual content (that is, to all kinds of library materials); the retrieval and dissemination of information, and the provision of information services; advanced training, such as the successful completion of a graduate program in library and information science;[5] and the intellectual skills required to plan and maintain collections of materials, to provide for their bibliographic and physical access, and to develop programs for the use and conservation of the materials and the dissemination of the information associated with the collection. Without citing educational specifics, a traditional and rather mechanical list of "suggested qualifications" for a museum librarian states:

> The Librarian administers the museum library and performs services such as selection, acquisition, cataloging, classification, circulation and maintenance of library materials; and furnishes reference, bibliographic and reader's advisory services. The librarian may have special responsibilities such as slides or graphics collections.[6]

But librarianship consists of more than such a to-do list. Obviously, one of the difficulties encountered in establishing the professional stance of librarians is the necessity of performing what appear to be marginally professional tasks—

a necessity certainly not unknown to other professions. The question of which activities and tasks are professional and which are clerical has been much debated in and out of association conferences. Many librarians feel that sharing their expertise enhances, rather than diminishes, it and that a professional task is anything that makes the library more effective.

Ideally, then, the museum library is headed by a professional librarian; certainly the museum board or trustees will attempt to secure the best person possible for the position. The librarian is responsible for what goes on in the library:

- Establishing and codifying the library mission and goals
- Researching and writing collection development policy, and applying that policy to acquisitions and collection management
- Determining the allocation and use of space within the library
- Planning and setting up procedures and processes such as shelf preparation of materials and production of catalog records
- Planning and supervising training for library staff, including volunteers
- Constructing catalog primary access (main entry) records
- Conducting data retrieval and performing information services beyond rudimentary reference questions, including information searches in other libraries and collections
- Assisting readers in database and Internet searching, and helping them evaluate what they retrieve
- Planning and supervising patron and end-user instruction
- Planning and developing programs, including the research prior to instituting new programs
- Planning and conducting staff and program assessment and evaluation
- Preparing and planning budgets, making annual reports, and assuming general fiscal responsibility for the operation of the library

In addition, the librarian must become "a student of the organization,"[7] realistically aware of the library's place within it; must be thoroughly familiar with the philosophy and methodology of museums; must know the mission, staff, and programs of the particular museum; and also must have an extensive knowledge of its subject-matter.

The ability to leap over tall buildings, while a useful skill, is not a reasonable expectation, even though the foregoing lists might suggest otherwise.

The Staff

The museum librarian will delegate activities to the library staff—when there is a staff.

"OPL." When the librarian is both librarian—that is, manager—and library staff, we have the OPL, or one-person library.[8] The situation, of course, is not uncommon in museum libraries. Robert G. Krupp's survey of science museum libraries indicated that not quite 40 percent employed a professional librarian, who most often served as a one-person staff.[9] Taking exception to the *one-person* term, Herbert S. White claims that *one-professional library* is more accurate.[10] *One-person* has probably been in use too long to change readily; nonetheless, we shall understand the "person" to be a professional whenever museum resources permit.

In the for-profit sector of special librarianship, the one professional of the OPL is likely to be the only library staff member; in museums and other not-for-profit organizations, where the staffing is more likely to be flexible and subject to alternatives, the one professional may be assisted by other people, including volunteers.

Library Assistants. Library assistants tend to be part-time, whether hourly employees or volunteers. They may have designated duties and assignments, or may cover the hours the librarian has duties elsewhere. Whatever the circumstances and assignments, they are invaluable and library services would be severely curtailed without them. Nor should there be any distinctions made between paid and volunteer library assistants; the volunteers are as much library staff as the paid persons and should be given the same opportunities for job satisfaction and development.

For the librarian, a management issue is piecing together bits and pieces of time and people to create a coherent staffing pattern and cohesive staff. There is also the scheduling havoc that results from any deviation in the pattern. (The background and experience provided by car-pooling or bowling-team scheduling is useful.)

As a rule, library assistants have specific duties and responsibilities to be carried out within a particular time slot or for a specific person. The tasks may include filing cards "above the rod" (that is, before the retaining rod is run through the holes), circulation and service desk duty, or card production from cataloging copy.

Library assistants should be familiar with the library's policies and procedures, the general location of materials, and the use of such tools as periodical indexes and the catalog. This requirement means that library assistants, whether volunteer or paid staff, will receive extensive training, just as museum docents partake in training programs. This staff training is a large aspect of the librarian's responsibilities.

A word about volunteers: Volunteering is an American tradition that makes possible many of the services non-profit and cultural organizations provide to their communities. But the demographic profile of volunteers is changing, and so is the role traditionally assigned to the unsalaried staff.[11] With more women in paid positions, there are fewer housewives to fill in working-day volunteer slots; but at the same time, more professionals are offering their labors to the community's agencies, especially the men and women employed in companies that encourage employee participation in local organizations. Also, as the active life span increases, retirees, eager to be useful, are seeking meaningful post-work occupations. High school and college students, particularly as they cast about for career direction or seek to fulfill social service obligations for graduation, also present themselves as volunteers.

In recruiting such volunteers, most of whom tend to be mindful of the value of their time, the librarian should stress the challenge and importance of library and information services.[12] As noted before, the only difference between the volunteer and paid staff member is that the paycheck received by the latter comes from the museum. In training, responsibilities, and expectations, the two groups are alike. Indeed, some organizations identify the internal department affiliation rather than signifying *volunteer* on identification badges.

If the museum has a tradition of volunteer luncheons, awards, or other formalized expressions of appreciation, the library's volunteers should, of course, participate. But an atmosphere of respect for the person and sincerely expressed appreciation, together with the opportunity to make a contribution are the major incentives of the workplace, for volunteers as well as for paid workers.[13] And satisfied, fulfilled volunteers become the library's best recruitment strategy.

Library Committee. A library committee, usually as an arm of the museum board or of a guild or auxiliary organization, is not unusual in museums. The committee should be an advocacy group, a cohort of advisers and volunteers. However, it should *not* be vested with an administrative role. If the library is to serve the mission of the museum, it must be organizationally under the board and museum administration, just as is any other department in the museum. The library committee, then, is not empowered to hire the librarian or library staff, make decisions regarding facilities, equipment, procedures or services, nor to undertake programs, acquisitions, or catalogs.

Staffing Alternatives

The museum administration has several staffing alternatives to consider in ensuring professional direction for the library when the museum is not able to employ a professional librarian on a full-time basis. There are two overriding considerations in all these staffing options:

First, the library requires an advocate who will attend museum staff meetings on the same basis as other department administrators and who will speak for the library formally and informally;

Second, the library needs a professional administrator who is able to develop collections and services in conjunction with the mission and needs of the museum.

It is best, but not absolutely necessary, that these roles be filled by the same person.

Half-time Professional. Next-best to a full-time professional is a half-time professional librarian who can develop a staff of well-trained library assistants capable of carrying out directives and policies.

Volunteer Professional. Another alternative to full-time professional help is a volunteer professional—a scarce commodity, save for the retiree pool. However, unless the volunteer professional is able to devote the equivalent of half-time employment, it is difficult to establish continuity and leadership. In addition, the combination of intermittent presence and unsalaried status invites psychological, if not administrative, circumvention on the part of patrons and library staff.

Museum Staff Member. A museum staff member is often selected (or self-selected) to organize and supervise the library. As already noted, this person used most often to be the head of the education department in the museum, and the library was, at least initially, one of the department's programs, along with school visits, lecture series, and outreach. In the decade between the early 80s and the middle 90s, the educator became displaced as the *de facto* librarian by registrars, curators, and even administrators.[14]

Whatever the other hat worn by the museum staff member, that person, when fulfilling the role of librarian, is responsible for the areas and activities listed above, while trained library assistants and volunteers deal with the daily operations and undertakings. However, if the staff member is not trained in librarianship and cannot construct a bibliographic record (much less teach someone else how to do it), then the museum must turn to professional guidance from consultants.

Consultants. In the absence of on-site professional guidance, the library may engage the services of a consultant, particularly in the starting-up period, to advise on goals, policies, and procedures. Staff training, budget development, and program planning are other areas a consultant may address.

For the protection of all parties, the consultancy should be on a contractual basis. The contract may call for bringing the consultant back at stated intervals to help evaluate staff performance and the information services and to plan the implementation of new programs or services.

Consultant services are offered by librarians and information scientists acting as independent contractors. Sometimes they call themselves information brokers. The telephone book may also list them under information services, information specialists, or library research services. They also advertise in the national library press, although a local specialist might enter into a more flexible and lengthy contract. The Special Libraries Association maintains a list of members who are able to serve as consultants. The public library staff also may be a source of information regarding local independent information specialists.

If the museum library is to find a volunteer consultant, the volunteer is not generally regarded as a library staff member. Rather, the assistants who are trained become the staff, while the library leadership is vested in a full-time museum staff member.

In turning to consultants, the library reaps the benefits of professional knowledge and insights and, at the same time, the stabilizing effects of full-time on-site presence—even though the staff member holds other duties and responsibilities. (The division of time and effort should be clearly delineated in a document approved by the administration and, if necessary, the board.)

It is, of course, unreasonable to expect staff of the local public library to advise in the administration of the museum library. They can supply printed resources and materials and specific data or information; they cannot be consultants except on their own time and after hours. If a school of library and information science is located nearby, its faculty members are in a similar position. Sometimes library science students will volunteer for the experience. Students, however, cannot be expected to assume professional responsibilities or to undertake an internship or work-study program unless a full-time professional is in charge.

Professional Development and Continuing Education

Personal and Professional Development. Sylvia Martin, in her keynote address to a conference of library assistants, stressed the concept that a career "is a time-extended working out of a purposeful life pattern through work undertaken by an individual." She further stated that there is "no career development without self-development."[15] Professional development and self-development, then, are as valid and vital for the library assistant as for the librarian, and even the active professional feels the need to explore a particular aspect of the field, to acquire new knowledge or update skills.

There are many ways to achieve professional development: through workshops sponsored by library and subject-oriented associations; through the conferences of these organizations; and through the continuing education programs sponsored by associations, schools of library and information science, and colleges and universities. Schools of library science, library associations, local and state professional groups, local libraries, and consortia of local or regional libraries are all sources of seminars, courses, workshops, and demonstrations.

The museum librarian should be on the mailing lists of these various sponsoring organizations.

The Special Libraries Association, as a national organization and through its regional chapters and subject-oriented divisions, is active in sponsoring continuing education and professional development. The Art Libraries Society of North America (ARLIS/NA) and the Society of American Archivists (SAA) sponsor continuing education at their conferences, while the American Association of Museums, the American Association for State and Local History, and subject-focus organizations such as the National Audubon Society and the National Trust for Historic Preservation offer conference workshops, short courses, and self-guided courses.

Planning for professional development and for any necessary continuing education is the responsibility of each staff member, but a responsibility shared with the librarian and the museum administration. Research has shown that museum librarians find that lack of funds and inability to arrange time away from work are the major impediments to participation in continuing education.[16] By extending to the library staff the same cost-sharing agreements and freed-up time arrangements received by other museum staff, the museum board supports the library and its contribution to the museum's mission.

Performance Evaluation—sometimes called personnel evaluation—is an aspect of professional development often lost in the not-for-profit shuffle. Yet benchmarks of progress are as necessary for people as for programs. The library should be linked with the museum's overall staff evaluation program, if there is one, and may also want to develop evaluations for its own staff as well.

Evaluation of staff must be objective: ideally, the **performance**, not the person, is evaluated on the basis of reality tests just as programs are. In service organizations such as museums and libraries, where there are no widgets to count, "concrete, measurable" standards are difficult to construct, and the constantly changing job picture means the standards must change to conform.[17] As Belcaster points out, the observation "Speaks in a friendly manner" is a better standard than the subjective "Has a friendly personality."[18]

Some staff members are comfortable with performance standards arrived at in consultation with the librarian; others prefer to develop their own performance objectives according to their roles and skills. Thus a performance goal of "checking in all magazines within an hour with no mistakes" may be a more meaningful goal to the periodicals assistant than "to enhance performance to .01 error," particularly when the assistant perceives the direct connection between fast, accurate work and the ability of the museum staff to obtain recent and essential information. The library staff needs to know that performance evaluations are not staff-weeding tools, but rather contribute to their professional development and to the museum's ability to do its work.

Planning

There is a role for serendipity in organizations, but it is sound planning that makes it possible to exploit the serendipitous occasion. Having a planned use for the unexpected gift, being able to give museum staff self-instructional packets for using the clipping file database, rescheduling volunteers in anticipation of an increase in telephone reference queries—these actions are not happenstances, but based on plans developed prior to the need. Planning, however, does not cover every contingency in the library day. Enough occurs unexpectedly under the best of planning conditions to make each day interesting.

The documents underlying all library planning are the museum's mission statement and the library's response in the forms of its goals. From the goals flow the objectives, and planning is necessary for the execution of these objectives.

Some authors make a distinction between program planning and strategic planning[19]—between planning for programmatic activities (such as teaching staff about using indexes) and planning for methods and processes (such as beginning to use card production software).[20] Perhaps the distinction is less important than knowing there are different kinds of planning and different purposes for plans.[21] Planning, in any case, takes into account the interrelationship of all possible variables—mission, resources, facilities, policies, public—in a future orientation.[22]

Planning is conducted with a *measurable* outcome in mind. If a goal is to serve the museum members' needs for environmental information, an appropriate objective would be "Within three months to be able to give two-day service on 95 percent of all appropriate environmental reference and data queries." Then the planning to achieve this successful response rate takes place in a series of steps: surveying members' probable environmental information needs (what's in the newspaper?), evaluating the usefulness of the reference collection and online services, tabulating the type of questions now being asked, assessing staff capabilities and planning training, surveying outside resources such as other libraries, and so on.

As each activity in the plan is set up, performed, and evaluated, the results indicate whether the plans are on the right track or whether some adjustments need to be made. It may become clear, for example, that 90 percent of queries can be answered within 24 hours, but, because of poor email connections with the biology library at Downstate University, the remaining 5 percent take nearly a week for response. The objective can then be restated more realistically and reference service evaluated on the adjusted basis.

Planning a ready reference service may lead to the purchase of duplicate materials when, for example, planning shows a basic reference tool will be in constant use by a curator but will also be needed by the rest of the library's patrons. The objective in this case is to satisfy the immediate needs of both the curator and the patrons.

Evaluation, or reality testing, is built into the planning process to the extent that the final rating of a program should be highly predictable. On-going evaluation is akin to videotaping the docents' presentation of a new exhibit. Evaluation may include test-runs of queries to the biology library or a mail survey of members to measure their awareness of the museum library's information services. Final, or program, evaluation is the summation of the quantifiable measures stated in the objective or objectives for the program; it is in that sense also a measurement of the planning process.

Planning also helps the library staff answer questions about the future. It is an essential tool when budget review comes around.

Budgets

The budget is, in effect, a plan for allocating resources to departments, functions, programs, or areas within an organization.[23] We shall assume the parent organization has a budget and budget process, and that the library is at least a line item on the museum budget, going through the same budget review and process as the other departments.

The library often receives gifts, especially memorials. Such gifts are earmarked as set-asides. They are designated augmentations of the library budget, and the amount of the gifts should not be subtracted from the budget.

There are several sorts of budgets, of varying degrees of complexity and usefulness to the museum library. The budgets most often encountered are the line item, and the programming.

Line Item Budget. The line item budget is the most straightforward, and most familiar.[24] As the term implies, the items for which the institution expects to spend its money are listed along with the amount of anticipated expenditure. If the library is a line item in the museum's budget, the various expenditures proposed for the library are listed and, when added up, equal the amount on the museum's budget line for the library.

Programming Budget. This is a more effective and informative budget, and one which is closely keyed to the library's planning. Rather than listing kinds of expenditures (supplies or postage, for example), the programming budget apportions expenditures to the various functions and activities supported by the library. Proposed expenditures for supplies may then be divided among cataloging and preparation, member information services, staff information services, and outreach; expenditures for postage, for example, will be divided among member services, cataloging and preparation, interlibrary loan, and outreach.

The programming budget thus demonstrates clearly the extent to which objectives are being supported and resources allocated to services established in the library's goals. It is possible, indeed, to construct an objective-based programming budget. Appendix F contrasts a line-item budget with a programmatic budget to demonstrate the differences in approach.

The programming budget is no more complicated to construct than the traditional line-item form. If the museum administration requires departmental budgets to be submitted in line form, a programming budget is still valuable to the library staff in the on-going evaluation process. And even if the museum does not require any budget document from the library, it is in the interests of the library and information services to develop a resources allocation plan to show how the various functions, activities, and programs will be supported.

A programming budget can be an enlightening document for those administrators who view the library simply as a place to store books. Hence, the librarian who has gone through the planning that precedes the development of a programming budget and the monitoring of expenditures as they occur can present a strong, documented case when seeking increases in resources, space, personnel, or programs.

Fees and charges. The matters of budgets and gifts also brings up the issue of fees, not one easily resolved within the museum profession. Whether the museum is perceived as a social good (with entrance the equivalent of a public library card), as a quasi-educational agency, or as higher-order entertainment, it is difficult for the museum community to observe Disney World and Six Flags and not dream a bit. Many museums, of course, charge entrance fees (or ask for donations), which, according to some researchers, result in "declining numbers of walkins."[25] But does what happens at the museum door apply also to the library?

Some museum libraries offering well-established and unique research programs are able to charge for research, document reproduction, and—to non-members—facility-use fees. An example is the Naeseth Library of the Vesterheim Norwegian-American Museum in Madison, Wisconsin. The fee schedule is stated in printed materials and on its page of the museum's Web site, http://www.vesterheim.org/genealogy.[26]

But the free tradition is strong among librarians and library users. While cost recovery for such services as photocopying is usually accepted, use fees and research charges generally are not. Service fees, however, are an avenue the well-established library might wish to explore—not so much as a means of income as of recovering certain operational costs such as photocopying, and telecommunication charges involved in research by Internet or long-distance telephone. However, before any schedule of charges goes forth, the library staff will need to deal with the attendant philosophical and ethical issues, taking their conclusions to the museum administration and board.

In order to charge fees, the library must have something to sell that the public knows about and desires and that cannot be otherwise obtained. How this comes about is part of the library staff's marketing program.

Marketing the Library

Librarians, like others in the not-for-profit service sector, tend to hold two myths: If we build it they will come, and Marketing is the same as manipulation.

The first myth dissolves when we have to ask, "We built it. Where are they?" This questio might never be posed if we can preempt it with the following: First, who are "they" and what will they do when they get here? Second, how will they know what we have built? "They" (we hope) are library users we want to reach (though we don't quite know who they are), and (we suppose) they will do whatever they are wont to do in libraries, when they know what we built. These speculations address the second myth, marketing.

Some Marketing Principles

There is more in the literature recently about marketing museums than their libraries, although authors sometimes mention the library as a potential marketing tool.[27] However, the marketing principles explicated for other not-for-profit agencies can also be applied to the museum library.

Marketing, so goes the myth, is the insidious, if not invidious, manipulation of people so that they act against their will and welfare. That may be a statement about propaganda; it is not about marketing. Rather, marketing is a matter of developing a product or service that will be beneficial to people—usually specific people—and then informing them about where it is available and how it will help them. This means that

> [a]n organization with a marketing orientation feels that its major task is a multifaceted one: to systematically study customer needs, wants, preferences and satisfaction levels; to redesign all elements of its products that are not satisfactory; to appropriately price and distribute these products; and to communicate their value to customers.[28]

Certainly these tasks—especially the first—apply to the special library:

> The first critical prerequisite for any marketing activity is an understanding of your customers and what they consider to be valuable and important.[29]

These tasks suggest some very concrete actions for the library staff to undertake both during the planning stages and after library operations have begun.

- Know the museum staff members, their jobs, their responsibilities; be aware of their current and future projects, their methods, and their information needs.[30] Know their learning styles (e.g., do they read about a topic, or do they telephone a colleague?). Let the data from coffee-break conversations and an information audit influence collection development.

- Determine what sorts of information services most suit their needs, a factor in planning and setting priorities for those services.

- Find out why those who express indifference to libraries feel that way; nonusers are an important library constituency. Think in terms of taking the library to them. (See discussion of cost, below.)

- Policies are necessary, but people are important. Walk in the patron's shoes: buy two copies of an often-sought title; extend the loan period; hand-deliver a new acquisition to the person who requested it.

- And remember: Library service for the user is the right information for the right person at the right time at the right price for the users' needs.[31] There is a simple cost equation that applies to life and equally to libraries: Satisfaction—Cost > 0.

In other words, patron satisfaction should be greater than the costs—in time, energy, and frustration—incurred by the patron in using library services. So if—perhaps because of the library's location—a major cost to the library user is the time involved in getting there, then the library staff's planning for and promoting library services might include prompt response to telephone inquiries.

Some Marketing Strategies

Promotion is part of marketing, a "creative strategy."[32] It means developing a name recognition and making sure library users—current and potential—have basic information about the library and its services. Here are some suggestions that have worked for museum libraries:

- Develop a logo and distinctive color scheme and use them on everything—letterhead, bookplates, memos, signs, whatever.[33] (A word of warning here: test market the logo and color scheme, make the logo simple and direct, and avoid garish or unusual colors.)

- If any library services—such as telephone reference or reading room use—will be available to museum members or the public, be sure the library, together with its telephone number, is mentioned in all museum brochures and printed pieces. If the piece shows a site map, have the location of the library indicated.

- Be sure the library and its location are included on museum informational signs. Have directional signs to the library placed wherever the visitor must decide on a change in direction.

- Have the library included as a link on the museum Web page. Bells and flashing lights are not necessary; display the logo and list hours and services available.[34] You may even plan to eventually make the catalog accessible from the museum's Web site.

- Plan "Open House events to publicize your institution's anniversaries, and other events such as National Archives Week, Museum Week, etc., ... and to coincide with anniversaries and birthdates" of persons associated with the museum's subject area or the library's collections.[35]

- Display interesting items from the collection near the museum entrance, along with a sign saying, "You'll find it in the Library."

- Cultivate and encourage suggestions from library users; have a suggestion box by the door; be alert to the most indirect and oblique offering; and respond to on all suggestions, even those that cannot be acted upon because of resources or policies.

- Celebrate gifts, volunteers' service, and library milestones such as a new online service.

- Use library posters wherever you can.

- Never turn down an opportunity to speak to community groups about the museum; introduce yourself as the librarian and briefly explain what you do.

- Engage the interest of the rest of the museum: have an active suggestion box; respond promptly to suggestions and incorporate them when feasible.

- Write up something interesting about the library for each issue of the museum's newsletter.

- Introduce yourself and your staff at every opportunity: staff meetings, board meetings, docent meetings, guild meetings.

- Be active in local library circles. Accept SLA office; you thereby promote your museum and your library—not to mention yourself.

Marketing, like planning and budgeting, is an on-going effort requiring review and evaluation, flexibility and creativity, and the firm belief on the part of the library staff in the value of the library to the museum.

In Summary

Before a museum library can successfully serve the parent institution, the staff must first decide how best (and who best) to carry out the goals and responsibilities adopted, how to maintain efficient and effective service, and how to reach out to potential patrons.

Starting-Up and Revitalizing

Several administrative principles should be observed from the beginning of the museum library:

1. All museum library administration—staffing, planning and budgeting—begins with the *museum's mission* and the *library's supporting goals and objectives.*

2. The *library staff*—librarian and assistants—compose goals and policies in conformity to the museum policies as set by the board. Someone, then, must be in *charge* of the daily operation of the library and bear the responsibility for its collection and information services. The museum library has various alternatives for leadership and staff. *Volunteers* are considered staff also, with opportunities for performance evaluation and professional development. Library staff members need opportunities for training and professional development and for a realistic evaluation of their performance.

3. *Planning* begins with the library's objectives. We can measure the success of plans as we measure the results of objectives. Planning and evaluation are both parts of a continuing process in the library.

4. The museum library should have a *budget* and a *dedicated, predictable income.* Even though it may be a line-item in the overall museum budget, the library can express its own plans and allocation of resources to those plans by developing a programming budget for internal use.

5. The library should have a *marketing program* based on present and future plans for services, and should take every opportunity to tell museum staff, administration, and members what is being offered and what is planned for the future. Suggestions from the library's constituency must be welcomed and acted on when within reason and the realm of resources, possibility, and budget.

Notes

1. For example, several directors stated that their museums did not have a library, yet I received survey responses from librarians at those institutions. See Esther Green Bierbaum, "The Museum Library Revisited," *Special Libraries* 75/4 (April 1984): 102–113.

2. Thomas Petzinger, Jr., "A New Model for the Nature of Business: It's Alive!" *The Wall Street Journal* 233/40 (26 February, 1999): B1, B4.

3. Linda M. McFadden, and Kay Hubbard, "Team Concepts for Emerging Organizational Architectures," *Information Outlook* 2/12 (December 1998): 18–23.

4. Esther Green Bierbaum, "Museum Libraries: The More Things Change...," *Special Libraries* 87/2 (Spring 1996): 74–87.

5. The educational criterion is not an absolute: both the American Library Association and the Special Libraries Association admit members who have "practiced in the capacity" of librarian for a certain number of years or who have had equivalent education and experience. The issue of librarians and professionalism does not go away quietly. For example, the librarian of Congress is not a librarian, and court cases have tested the validity of the professional qualifications (*Merwine v. Board of Trustees for State Institutions of Higher Learning* [Mississippi], **754 2d 631, 5th Circuit, 1985**).

6. Janet W. Solinger, ed., *Museums and Universities: New Paths for Continuing Education* (New York: National University Continuing Education Association, 1990), p. 303.

7. A phrase readily attributed to Edward Gallion Holley, Dean Emeritus of the School of Information and Library Sciences, University of North Carolina at Chapel Hill, and uttered on innumerable occasions.

8. Guy St. Clair and Joanne Williamson, *Managing the New One-Person Library*, 2nd ed. (New York; London: Bowker Saur, 1992.)

9. Robert G. Krupp, "Small Science Museum Libraries: Remarks on a Sampling of Data," *Science and Technology Libraries* 6 (Fall 1985-Winter 1986): 91–101.

10. Herbert S. White, "Basic Opportunities and the Pursuit of Equal Opportunity, Part 1," *Library Journal* 113/12 (July 1988): 56.

11. Peter F. Drucker, "The Non-Profits' Quiet Revolution," *The Wall Street Journal* (8 September 1988): A22.

12. Joan Kuyper *et al.*, *Volunteer Program Administration: A Handbook for Museum and Other Cultural Institutions* (New York: American Council for the Arts, 1993).

13. Thomas J. Peters and Robert H. Waterman, *In Search of Excellence: Lessons from America's Best-Run Companies* (New York: Harper and Row, 1982), pp. 238–239.

14. Bierbaum, "Museum Libraries," p. 70.

15. Sylvia Cooke Martin, "Keynote Address...Conference of Library Assistants," *Journal of Education for Library and Information Science* 28/4 (Spring 1988): 259–261.

16. Esther Green Bierbaum, "Museums, Arts and Humanities Librarians: Careers, Professional Development and Continuing Education," *Journal of Education for Library and Information Science* 29/2 (Fall 1988): 127–134.

17. Carol F. Goodson, *The Complete Guide to Performance Standards for Library Personnel* (New York: Neal-Schuman, 1997), pp. 17, 18; Jonathan A. Lindsey, ed., *Performance Evaluation: A Management Basic for Librarians* (Phoenix, Ariz.: Oryx, 1986).

18. Patricia Belcaster, *Evaluating Library Staff: A Performance Appraisal System* (Chicago: ALA, 1998), p. 7.

19. Robert N. Anthony, and David W. Young, *Management Control in Nonprofit Organizations*, 6th. ed. (Burr Ridge, Illinois: Irwin/McGraw-Hill, 1999), p. 353.

20. Doris Asantewa, *Strategic Planning Basics for Special Libraries* (Washington, D.C.: SLA, 1992.)

21. For examples of formal planning documents, see *Planning for Library Excellence* (Richmond: Virginia State Library and Archives, 1988); *The Planning Process* (Chicago: ALA, 1988); and Ethel E. Himmel, William J. Wilson, and the ReVision Committee of the Public Library Association, *Planning for Results: a Public Library Transformation Process* (Chicago: ALA, 1998).

22. Donald E. Riggs, *Strategic Planning for Library Managers* (Phoenix, Ariz.: Oryx, 1984), pp. 2–3.

23. For the librarian who opted out of Accounting 101, see Alice Sizer Warner, *Budgeting: A How-to-Do-It Manual for Librarians* (New York: Neal-Schuman, 1998.)

24. Herbert S. White, *Managing the Special Library: Strategies for Success Within the Larger Organization* (White Plains, N.Y.: Knowledge Industry Publications, 1984), pp. 89, 92–93.

25. Victoria Dickensen, "The Economics of Museum Admission Charges," *Curator* 36/3 (1993): 220–234.

26. The library of the Bishop Museum (Hawaii) instituted a fee in March 1999 for non-members and persons who have not paid a museum admission, reporting little or no resistance, and no effect on patron numbers. Personal correspondence, 5 September 1999.

27. Fiona McLean, *Marketing the Museum* (London and New York: Routledge, 1997), p. 112.

28. Sharon L. Baker, *The Responsive Public Library Collection: How to Develop and Market It* (Englewood, Col.: Libraries Unlimited, 1993), p. 16.

29. Christine A. Olson and Suzanne Stewart Moseman, "Don't Stop Marketing!" *Information Outlook* 1/3 (March 1997): 20–23.

30. N. Shillinglaw, "Public Relations and Museum Libraries," *Mousaion* 4/1 (1986): 77–84.

31. Maryde F. King, "The Marketing Approach Applied to Special Libraries in Industry: A Review of the Literature," *Science and Technology Libraries* 6/1-2 (Fall 1985-Winter 1986): 119–152.

32. Thomas H. Aageson, "Market Value: 5 Steps to an Effective Museum Marketing Plan," *Museum News* 78/4 (July/August 1999): 36–37, 56–63.

33. For suggestions, both philosophical and practical, see John Kirby, *Creating the Library Identity: A Manual of Design* (Aldershot, Hants (England); Brookfield, Vermont: Gower, 1985).

34. Of the 15 Web sites I checked in July and August 1999—for museums I knew had libraries—only two listed that library on the home page, while four others made it a second or third page link under "Services" or "Information."

35. Patricia Pettijohn, Poynter Library, University of South Florida, St. Petersburg, personal communication.

Further Reading

Staff

Belcaster, Patricia. *Evaluating Library Staff: A Performance Appraisal System*. Chicago: ALA, 1998.

Carmichael, David W. *Involving Volunteers in Archives*. S.l.: Mid-Atlantic Archives Conference, 1990.

Fischer, Lucy Rose, and Kay Bannister Schaffer. *Older Volunteers: A Guide to Research and Practice*. London: Sage, 1993.

Goodson, Carol F. *The Complete Guide to Performance Standards for Library Personnel*. New York: Neal-Schuman, 1997.

Kuyper, Joan, with Ellen Cochran Hirzy and Kathleen Huftalen. *Volunteer Program Administration: A Handbook for Museum and Other Cultural Institutions*. New York: American Council for the Arts, 1993.

McFadden, Linda M., and Kay Hubbard, "Team Concepts for Emerging Organizational Architectures," *Information Outlook* 2/12 (December 1998): 18–23.

St. Clair, Guy, and Joan Williamson. *Managing the New One-Person Library*. 2nd ed. London; New York: Bowker Saur, 1992.

Planning

Anthony, Robert N., and David W. Young. *Management Control in Nonprofit Organizations*. 6th ed. Burr Ridge, Ill.: Irwin/McGraw-Hill, 1999.

Asantewa, Doris. *Strategic Planning Basics for Special Libraries*. Washington, D.C.: SLA, 1992.

Bremer, Suzanne W. *Long-Range Planning: A How-To-Do-It Manual for Public Libraries*. New York: Neal-Schuman, 1994.

Himmel, Ethel E., William J. Wilson, and the ReVision Committee of the Public Library Association. *Planning for Results: A Public Library Transformation Process*. Chicago: ALA, 1998.

Riggs, Donald E. *Strategic Planning for Library Managers*. Phoenix, Ariz.: Oryx, 1988.

Virginia State Library and Archives. *Planning for Library Excellence*. Richmond: The State Library, 1988.

Budgeting

Martin, Murray S. *Collection Development and Finance: A Guide to Strategic Library-Materials Budgeting*. Chicago: ALA, 1995.

_____, and Milton T. Wolf. *Budgeting for Information Access: Managing the Resource Budget for Absolute Access*. Chicago: ALA, 1998.

Turock, Betty J., and Andrea Pedolsky. *Creating a Financial Plan: A How-to-Do-It Manual for Librarians*. New York: Neal-Schuman, 1992.

Warner, Alice Sizer. *Budgeting: A How-to-Do-It Manual for Librarians*. New York: Neal-Schuman, 1998.

Marketing

Aageson, Thomas H. "Market Value: 5 Steps to an Effective Museum Marketing Plan." *Museum News* 78/4 (July/August 1999): 36–37, 56–6.

Baker, Sharon L. *The Responsive Public Library Collection: How to Develop and Market It*. Englewood, Colo.: Libraries Unlimited, 1993.

King, Maryde F. "The Marketing Approach to Special Libraries in Industry: A Review of the Literature." *Science and Technology Libraries* 6/1-2 (Fall 1985-Winter 1986): 119–152.

Kotler, Neil, and Philip Kotler. *Museum Strategy and Marketing: Designing Missions, Building Audiences, and Generating Revenue and Resources*. San Francisco: Josey-Bass, 1997.

McLean, Fiona. *Marketing the Museum*. London and New York: Routledge, 1997.

Olson, Christine A., and Suzanne Stewart Moseman. "Don't Stop Marketing!" *Information Outlook* 1/3 (March 1997): 20–23.

Talaga, James A. "Concept of Price in a Library Context." *Journal of Library Administration* 14/4 (1991): 87–101.

Wood, Elizabeth J. *Strategic Marketing for Libraries: A Handbook*. New York: Greenwood, 1988.

Chapter 6

Information Services:
Some Basics

Information Services:
The Why of the Library

The people, the place, and the planning, activities and procedures discussed in the preceding chapters have one purpose: to deliver the library's information services to those who need them.

The library may be managed by a professional librarian; it may be housed in a pleasant, uncrowded space, furnished with attractive, durable shelves, desks, and chairs and equipped with the tools necessary to function efficiently; it may have a large collection of materials judiciously selected to support the work of the museum administration and staff. But if the library does not provide information services, despite its other attributes, it has not gone beyond the storage concept.

On the other hand, the collection may be small and inadequately housed in a room lacking comfortable furniture or an attractive color scheme, but if the library can deliver accurate data and useful information in timely fashion to the museum staff and members, then the library is providing the information services that allow it rightfully to take its place in supporting the mission of the museum.

This chapter and the next describe and discuss the various kinds of information services the museum library may provide its constituency, together with suggestions on relating and offering the services to the various departments and units within the museum. Few libraries can support fully all the services; the mission of the museum, the information needs of staff and members, and the goals of the library will help determine those to be selected and those to be emphasized and developed. The services should be designed to make the work of the museum staff more efficient and more effective and may include reference and bibliographic services such as

1. Circulation of materials
2. Reference: Data and information sources
3. Data and information retrieval
4. Bibliographic services

These are fairly basic services and most libraries, including the paper-based, can offer at least two or three of them. Beyond these, the library may offer extended services such as

5. Specialized information delivery
6. Data analysis
7. Bibliographic and user instruction
8. Programs, exhibits, and research
9. Conservation and preservation
10. Archival services

Such extended services will be the subject of chapter 7.

The following functions and groups within the museum will be considered, when appropriate, in discussing the application of information services and extended services: the museum board and administration; the business office; the offices of membership, public relations and development; the departments of curation and registration; the offices of research, grants, and field study; the departments of exhibits and interpretation, and education, instruction, and docentry; the museum members; the area of outreach and the general public; and the museum and information professions.

In the small museum, of course, where one person embodies several roles — and usually at the same time — functions and responsibilities are not as neatly apportioned as this list of groups and functions might indicate. Neither does one museum, of whatever size, usually embrace all of these functions and groups in equal measure. Consequently, when we describe information services for a department or unit, it is with the understanding that one individual may be addressed in more than one role, and that functions in some museums may be subsumed under a larger heading or grouped in a different organizational structure.

An inevitable question will be, Who may claim what service? Decisions about service claims and priorities must be based on the museum's mission and goals and the realities of the library's resources. The decisions should also become part of the library's overall policy manual formulated in consultation with the museum administration and the museum staff as a whole. The policy manual is a published document, distributed to museum staff along with other institutional policies and statements.

But there are also political realities in the special library's provision of information services; for example, the board and administration, logically and by reason of organizational structure, can stake a high priority claim. As circumstances within and outside the museum change, and as the library and information services expand in resources and staff, the policies must be reviewed, rewritten, and redistributed. A primary task in library planning is matching, over time, the varieties of information services with the goals and needs of those associated with the museum.

Reference and Bibliographic Services

The museum library's information services provide both data (raw figures and isolated facts) and information (data given meaning by being placed in a context); *"information services"* is a generic term meant to convey both aspects. And while information services are most often and most conveniently based on the library's collection and the tools that unlock it, bibliographic and physical access to the carriers of data and information can extend well beyond the local walls.

The in-house service probably most often associated with libraries is that of circulation, the lending of library materials.

Circulation of materials

Chapter 3 has already treated circulation as the end-result of technical services. We now examine it as an information service offered almost invariably to museum staff, often to museum members, and seldom to the public.

Patrons tend to equate circulation with the loan of books, which are still the life blood of museum libraries. However, any materials in the library—any carriers of intellectual content—are potentially subject to loan and, therefore, to circulation policies. Consequently, when we speak of getting "books" into the hands of library users, we include all of the print and nonprint items in the collection that are portable and safe to loan.

Circulation is less of an overriding concern to special librarians than to librarians in academic or public libraries. Especially if circulation is limited to administration and staff, borrowers are a stable population in a circumscribed arena. Moreover, the special librarian knows the members of that population and their information needs so well that circulation holds few surprises. If, for example, the field staff is investigating a possible new species of freshwater crab, *Freshwater Crustaceans* may be reasonably presumed to be in their lab. Furthermore, it may as well stay there until and unless someone else needs it.

The real question is how important circulation *records* are in the museum library that circulates material only to staff. The situation is analogous to the registrar's object location records: while the registrar may carry the object collection in his or her head, it is still necessary to provide documentary guides to the location of any object at any time. In the same way, the librarian may have a good notion of the likely whereabouts of *Freshwater Crustaceans*, but that is a useful datum only if the librarian is there to divulge it.

Here is a practical suggestion that guides the librarian's actions and is only half-facetious: ***Act in all things as though someone else might have to take over after lunch***. That is, **record everything**.

In the library serving museum staff only, the circulation may well be open-ended as to length of loan, and informal as to procedures—as long as there is some written notation in a logical place. Three common methods of keeping circulation records are (1) book cards that are signed and filed with each transaction; (2) a transaction log that is kept by the library or library assistant; and (3) a sign-out sheet that is initialed by staff members.

Borrowing procedures should permit self-service during the hours the library is not staffed—hence the log is a part-time solution. The sign-out sheet violates the principle of borrower privacy. Thus the book card is the easiest paper-based circulation system to institute and maintain. When automation comes to the library, the computerized circulation system should also allow self-service for museum staff.

In terms of day-to-day use of the collection, if the museum staff perceives the record of borrowing as simply a way of keeping track of library materials for the convenience of everyone, rather than as a librarian-devised method of attaching a short leash to favorite resources, compliance is usually not a problem. And if a curator is in too great a hurry to deal with circulation procedures, then it is easier for the librarian to make a notation than to delay or interrupt the course of research. After all, the museum library is there to support, not hinder or impede, the functions and activities of the museum.

When museum members are added to the borrowing population, the circulation procedures necessarily become more stringent and formalized—at least for the off-site segment of the population. The library must devise a circulation system, using museum membership cards or museum library cards, and develop circulation policies covering length of loan and means for recall. Because of the complications introduced by extending circulation privileges to members, many museum libraries restrict the collection to in-library use or confine circulation to certain days or hours of the day.

If the membership office feels that library privileges are a membership selling point and the library cooperates in offering those privileges, the library staff must ensure that the needs of the museum administration and staff are met first, and that the collection can support the interests of members.

Interlibrary loan (ILL). When the library's collection cannot meet a patron's need, the librarian can turn to ILL. Interlibrary Loan, as the name implies, is the cooperative library system whereby resources are shared among libraries. Members of bibliographic utility networks such as OCLC and RLIN are members also of an ILL network. The whole system of ILL is based on the realities of present-day economics and availability of resources and is reinforced by the growing realization among librarians that "access" must also mean "we can get it for you somewhere." For the library patron, this reality means that "now" is often "as soon as possible."

There are various reasons for turning to ILL: the library does not have the needed edition; the item was not purchased because there was little demand projected for it; the work is out of print and not available through normal market sources; the library's backfile of a journal title is not extensive enough; or circumstances in the museum or the museum world have brought the item into unexpected prominence. An example of this last circumstance was the demand for Rachel Carson's government publications after the success of her monographs.

Materials for ILL, particularly books, can be located through union catalogs and by inquiry to a likely library. If the librarian has access to OCLC or RLIN (the Research Libraries Network), holdings information for books and serials is available online. The *National Union Catalog* (NUC) also carries holdings information, some of it out of date.

Protocols for borrowing require the library to seek the needed item from nearby libraries. In fact, state library systems and regional systems or consortia usually have fairly strict hierarchies of inquiry.[1] The museum librarian who anticipates demand from museum staff beyond the limits of the collection and collection development policy should investigate the local and regional ILL networks. Costs, whether for mailing or for making photocopies, are borne by the borrowing library.

There are two matters to consider: first, a heavy use of ILL suggests the need for a reassessment of the collection development policy; second, by requesting materials through interlibrary loan, the museum library becomes a lender as well. The ILL functions should be written into library policies, and the museum board and administration should be aware of them.

All persons associated with the museum are potential beneficiaries of circulation services. However, the library may be hard put to support very many borrowing populations, especially in the beginning. Unless a survey of museum membership indicates otherwise and the board and membership department urge borrowing privileges as a membership perk, the library should concentrate on offering circulation and other services to the museum staff. Such a restriction obviously does not keep the library from being open to the general public for in-house use during certain hours.

Reference: Data and Information Sources

"Reference," in library-speak, harks back to the days of referring—pointing the patron in the direction of a source: "Fruit flies? Look in the insect book—the big green one—on the second shelf. And look under *D* for *drosophila*, not *F* for fruit flies."

The reference work carried out by the library staff now goes far beyond pointing to a likely source of data; but the term for the activity and the works containing the data still reflects the older methodologies.

Museum libraries offer reference services almost as often as reading room space, according to my surveys; and reference services are extended almost equally to museum staff, members, and the public.[2] Hence reference materials—print, nonprint, and database sources of data and information in museology and the museum's subject area—are essential to the library's collection. In fact, the beginning collection development policy will probably give priority to the acquisition of reference materials.

The reference materials should be handily and prominently displayed and arranged for maximum accessibility by browsing. Labeling the shelves, grouping reference sources by subject or type, and providing a quick list or index for reference materials are ways to speed the process of finding the right source.

Rather than being a pointer-out, the librarian is now the intermediary between the library patron who needs to know something (about fruit flies, say) and the reference sources in which that data may be found. This information transaction—the bringing together of information need and information source—is often of the quick reference variety: locating facts, figures, dates, pictures, and so on. Frequently the inquiry comes by telephone.[3]

Indeed, the museum library can develop a bond of community goodwill by being a fast and reliable source of data within the museum's subject-field. That kind of reputation depends upon a thorough knowledge of the materials in a sound, working reference collection. In the interests of efficient reference service *and* documenting the value of the library, the staff needs to record and index "non-trivial inquiries"—without, of course, identifying the inquirer.[4]

Reference sources and materials represent a large investment and should be selected carefully, with full regard to the library's support of the museum's mission. There are several basic selection criteria for reference materials. They should be

- *current* (the latest edition where possible),

- *authoritative* (written or compiled by experts in the field and published a well-known house),

- *accurate* (well-received by authoritative reviewers, a standard work in the field, or checked for accuracy by another expert),

- *legible* (particularly if there is tabular material),

- *well-illustrated* (where visual explanations are appropriate, colors should be accurate, scale indicated, and labels explicit); and, in the case of printed resources,

- *durably-bound* (able to withstand hard use).

To establish or update a reference collection, the beginning librarian should consult bibliographies and lists of reference works and resources in the museum's subject field. (See chapter 2, "Further Reading.") Subject experts on the museum staff, in other libraries, and in local college or university departments will also provide suggestions. Guides to the literature in the discipline or disciplines of interest are essential. The bibliographies published by associations also list standard reference works.

When reference materials are books, they are usually shelved as a separate, noncirculating collection and are coded *REF* on their spines. In the beginning, however, if the collection consists largely of reference materials and serves museum staff only, and if records are kept of book movement from place to place within the museum, distinctions among materials will not be useful. If a particular title used often in reference work by the librarian keeps finding its way to a curatorial office, then previously established collection policies will indicate the validity of purchasing a second copy for reference, and redubbing the first a circulating title.

In addition to the subject-specialized reference works, the reference collection should include an unabridged dictionary; appropriate foreign language dictionaries (French, Italian, and Spanish in the arts; German, Russian and probably Japanese in the sciences); a style manual; a general thesaurus; directories of museums, libraries and foundations; an atlas and an almanac; and—as appropriate—compendia of standard mathematical and statistical tables, chemical formulae, and equations in mechanics, physics, and astronomy.

Translations also are required from time to time. Commercial translation services, foreign language journals in translation, and English-language abstracts are all potential resources. The museum library whose patrons use foreign language materials can also develop a datafile of local translators, who may be located in college and university faculties (not necessarily in the language departments), through lists kept by local police departments and social service agencies, and among the membership of cultural and ethnic societies. Speed, accuracy, and cost are factors the librarian must consider in securing translation services. Translations and translation programs are now among Internet resources.

Reference materials may also appear in nonbook formats, such as field guides and taxonomic keys on plastic cards, catalogs on microfiche, or in nonprint formats such as time-line charts, posters, and three-dimensional objects in type collections of fabrics, minerals, tools, rocks, or plants. Computerized reference sources—such as databases on disks (either prepared commercially or created in-house) and on CD-ROMs—are widely used, and the space-saving and multimedia attributes of this technology have attracted the notice of publishers of encyclopedias, indexes, thesauri, and other reference works.[5]

All of the museum departments and functions are served by the reference collection. To the extent of limitations imposed by board policy, the public may also consult the materials, which implies, of course, that the library staff will also be consulted. If telephone quick reference services are offered by the library, then it is difficult to justify denying the same services to those who ask in person.

Data and Information Retrieval

Once upon a time, after the librarian had pointed out a source, the burden of finding the information fell upon the patron. Retrieval, however, is a cooperative effort between librarian and patron, beginning with the interview in which they mutually determine the nature and scope of the patron's information quest and then proceed to examine the print and nonprint sources that may yield the information.

Special librarians work hard to develop and refine their interview skills; when properly conducted, the interview saves time, effort, and frustration for librarian and patron alike. The careful interview also permits the librarian and patron to modify and shape the search as new lines of approach suggest them-selves.[6]

Retrieval, then, is distinct from reference; the assumption is that the source is not necessarily on the library's shelves, but may be sought beyond its walls:

> Any modern information centre does not attempt to be self-contained, but sees itself as an entry point to the network of the world's infor-mation resources.[7]

Reference and retrieval blend at the edges when reference extends beyond those walls, as with the use of that reference standby, the telephone. Calls to other museums, libraries, and organizations involved in the same subject-field may be the simplest and most direct way to answer a query. Newspaper libraries and morgues, headquarters of associations, and departments in colleges and univer-sities are also possible data sources. The librarian who tracks down information by telephone may expect to be on the receiving end of queries; indeed, the library should make known its unique reference resources and areas of expertise to other information services.

Online databases. Since their beginnings in the late 1960s, online databases have become a proliferating and important retrieval mechanism. Indeed, retrieval, in its current sense, usually implies a search of remote databases by telecom-munication connection.

Specialized databases, such as those maintained by the Center for Disease Control, the American Chemical Society, the Astronomical Union, the Getty Museum, and so on, are invaluable for the researchers in a subject specialty. These databases provide flexibility in combining index terms, as well as currency and speed that cause them to outshine searching for data in print sources.

Many data sources are available only electronically. Perhaps librarians who do not yet have access to online databases can comfort themselves that tele-connections to books don't become overloaded with competing traffic, and that once the book is purchased, a search is not an added expense.

And expense there is: the requisite components of online searching are the desktop or laptop computer with modem (i.e., telephone line connection), a direct connection to the database or time-sharing communication set-up, and a subscription or other contract arrangement with the database. All these compo-nents add up to monetary outlays the library must either recapture or for which it must budget.

Depending on the museum's budget structure, it may be possible to charge per-search costs to the department seeking the data. However, there are some options for securing online services without incurring all of the costs. For exam-ple, the librarian can structure the search (that is, select combinations of index-ing terms) and then have it executed at a subscribing library, to which direct charges would then be paid. Such alternatives are discussed in more detail in chapter 8.

Another way around online charges is to secure the database in CD-ROM format. Since datafiles such as encyclopedias, statistical sources, and bibliographical resources are purchased outright, like books, the cost uncertainties of online searching are mitigated. Some CD-ROM databases are sold with updates, but some degree of currency may be lost.

Even though being able to offer online searching is a distant dream in the beginning, online databases are important data retrieval sources, the end results highly regarded by library users. They are

> what the user in search of information especially wants: a not too expensive, legible photocopy of an article from a scientific journal on his desk within three or four days. All other forms of information supply which libraries *are able to* provide, appear to arouse less interest.[8]

The librarian should be aware of various retrieval options, suggesting such a search and the means of accomplishing it when the situation warrants.

Online retrieval also includes the *Internet*, with its vast and proliferating array of information-bearing pages and links—information which, like any other data source, must be evaluated for currency, reliability, and validity.[9] Internet access includes, of course, the prerequisites of computer, modem, and connections, plus portal costs, all of which the library may well not have, especially in the beginning stages.

The Internet has been more of a do-it-yourself retrieval world; the myth has gone out that anyone with a browser and some keywords can find anything. When the patron discovers that this is not quite true, the librarian is called upon. It behooves the librarian to pay attention to the articles in the library literature that are filled with helpful advice designed to sharpen one's Internet skills.[10]

With the involvement of library staff in the search process, the retrieval of data and information becomes more costly in terms of staff time and is more likely to have policy restraints imposed. The special library, sponsored as it is by the constituency of the parent organization, may consider service allocation as part of strategic planning—that is, charging direct costs of searching to the department served.

All areas of the museum have a legitimate claim upon retrieval services, except, perhaps, museum members. This last group might be served on a staff availability basis, perhaps with a library assistant performing searches for members at set intervals, such as weekly. (Members who prefer faster turn-around can, of course, be encouraged to come in and use the printed indexes and reference materials for themselves.)

Because of cost factors, the general public may not be included as a beneficiary of the library's retrieval services. Such a decision will, naturally, be a matter of stated policy. Some libraries support substitutes such a call-in information service, which may be offered as part of the public relations and outreach programs. The service is designed to provide answers to the most common short and specific queries in the museum's subject-area. To answer typical data requests, such as snake and plant identification, local history dates, star and planet location, and common chemical equations, the library provides the data and their sources in an accessible format, such as an index card file or notebook.

In addition to forming a policy covering retrieval services for museum members and the general public, the library must decide how to handle information requests from other museums and libraries. This service is the sort of professional courtesy that similar organizations grant one another. Moreover, if the museum library has sought data or reference service from another library or is a network or consortium member, data reciprocity is ethically mandatory.

The costs of reference and retrieval service are considerable; it is one of the most labor-intensive aspects of library information services and merits strategic planning to increase efficiency and effectiveness. The librarian and library assistants should set objectives for reference service and establish performance measures of "fill rate" (percentage of queries answered), timeliness, and patron satisfaction.[11] Accuracy is another important and measurable aspect of this service; research has indicated that in some reference situations half the answers are wrong or did not address the original question.[12]

In the special library, the accuracy and usefulness of reference answers can be measured through surveys of the library's defined set of users. One of the frustrations of reference work is not knowing whether the answer really made a difference; museum librarians are in a position to research this question and to find out.

Actually, when it comes down to the costs of reference and retrieval services, the services based on print resources are usually not at issue; *reference* services such as locating facts, figures and pictures are part of the library tradition. However, because *online retrieval* services come with telecommunication charges, subscriptions charges, and a price tag on the print-out itself, retrieval costs become an issue.

In the corporate special library, online services are usually part of the corporation's or department's cost of doing business. In the not-for-profit organization, when such out-of-ordinary—and seemingly out-of-pocket—costs are incurred, a strong tendency arises to divorce those costs from the costs of print, and to look for substitutes where none exist, even when the library has a programming budget structured to show the allocation of costs to the museum functions which incur them. In time, however, online services may be regarded as legitimate costs of data retrieval in the same way as the purchase of new editions of the *CRC Handbook*.

The whole issue of cost and price applied to library services needs to be met forthrightly by the librarian and the museum administration, and then written into the library's policies. Charges, as Talaga points out, must be related to the goals and sponsorship of the library.[13] If the goal of the library is to support the research of the museum staff and the library is sponsored by the museum on behalf of its staff and mission, then online charges, like the price of books, are one of the costs of doing the work of the museum.

Bibliographic Services

There is a practical distinction among the terms, reference services, data retrieval, and bibliographic services. The first two instances have to do with locating data or information from print or other sources; the third has to do with *bibliography*, the records of information about publications and their location. In bibliographic services, the librarian secures and structures bibliographic information, often as a compendium (in the form of a bibliography) or by providing individual lists based on a search for books or periodical literature dealing with a specific topic or topics, or by a particular author. Such books or periodicals may either be in the library's collection or beyond the library's walls, but obtainable through interlibrary loan. The librarian then reports the results to the patron, perhaps including the outside sources: "Here are the books we have on this subject, and two others I can obtain from another library," or, "Here are the titles of three articles on your topic, but we don't have the journals. Do you want me to order photocopies from the holding libraries?"

Verification, both of books and journal articles, is an important aspect of bibliographic services. Tracking publication history, locating subsequent editions, checking footnotes for volume and page numbers—these are services often needed by the museum's researchers and professional staff members in preparing papers or searching the literature.

Book data. The salient data about books—author, title, place, publisher, and price—are found in printed bibliographies, including *Books in Print*, *Cumulative Book Index*, and the *National Union Catalog* (NUC), as well as specialized print bibliographies, such as guides to the literature of a discipline. Among online sources are the Library of Congress, bibliographical databases such as OCLC, RLIN, and WLN—and even online booksellers.

Serials data. The periodical literature, valuable for reporting findings before they appear in books, is indexed in several ways. We have looked at the online version of periodical data as an aspect of retrieval services. There are print sources as well. The principal printed indexes covering the periodical literature of the museum's subject matter should, in the absence of online capabilities, be part of the library's reference collection.

Museum literature is largely indexed in *Art Index;* humanities, in *Humanities Index;* and science—depending on intensity and depth of coverage—is found in *General Science Index, Science and Technology Index, Biological and Agricultural Index, Index Medicus, Biological Abstracts*, and the various forms of *Chemical Abstracts*, among others. Historical materials are indexed in *Social Science Index, Social Science Abstracts, Humanities Index*, and *Reader's Guide to Periodical Literature*.

The publisher of each index furnishes a list of the periodicals covered, but the librarian must select the index or indexes that best match the library's periodical holdings and the titles to which the library has access in other libraries. Newspaper indexes are also published.

These paper indexes are updated monthly or quarterly, and then bound annually. While they are now being supplanted by their CD-ROM and online versions, which offer faster updates and flexible searching beyond the author-title-subject access of the printed indexes, they have such as advantages as portability and the possibilities of serendipitous browsing.

Certainly the library should subscribe to a few highly pertinent paper indexes unless and until it achieves online capabilities. And meanwhile, the librarian should be aware of the electronic formats, since they are accessible in other libraries, and ought to be included in the museum library's long-range planning.

Staff in all departments and divisions of the museum will want to avail themselves of bibliographic services for both books and journals, whether single-title data ("Is there a second edition of this book?") or group data ("What was written last year about *Gymnodinium* toxin?"). Group data are often presented in bibliographies.

Bibliographies. Bibliographies are one of the most visible and popular information services the library can offer to the museum staff and to the membership and public. Depending on the need and the occasion, bibliographies may be on specific topics, may bring together materials reflecting divergent viewpoints, or may showcase a portion of the collection. Cooperative bibliographies list materials from the museum library as well as those located in the public or school library.[14] In compiling cooperative bibliographies, the library staff should take care to note clearly the location or locations of the items, together with their call numbers.

The compilation of bibliographies requires several skills. The librarian or library assistant must be thoroughly familiar with bibliographic formats;[15] be versed in the literature and literature sources of the subject in hand; and, knowing the readership and purpose of the bibliography, exercise judgment in the selections and annotations. Bibliographies should include audiovisual and other nonprint resources as a way of broadening the readers' awareness of information sources and of introducing the users to other parts of the library collection.

The librarian might keep in mind that length can be intimidating. Children especially are more comfortable with a single sheet of paper. If the bibliography runs longer than a page, the library staff should arrange the entries so that the high interest items are placed on the first page, with a "more about" supplement attached to it.

In addition to exercising judgment in selecting entries for the bibliographies, librarians should pay attention to the appearance of the entries on the page, art work, and paper color and weight. Desktop publishing software for personal computers offers great possibilities for creating interesting-looking, attractive, and readable bibliographies.

Some museum librarians have gone beyond bibliographies in forging the link between the museum's exhibits and programs and the library's materials and information services. Here one needs to develop imagination, élan, and a spirit of adventure. For example, tying into the rage for saurians and linking that interest to books and other media, the Children's Museum of Indianapolis has created Rex's Lending Center, presided over by a surprisingly benevolent Tyrannosaurus Rex.[16] With a closely defined selection of various media, the library makes an explicit connection between the library and the museum and the learning that takes place in each. The catalog for Rex's Lending Center is accessible from three of the museum's galleries, and materials can be reserved at the "Rexervation Station" for later pick-up and check-out. Thus, through book or tape, the young visitor can extend and savor the museum experience at home.

Of course, not every librarian is going to identify with saurians, no matter how worthy the bibliographic cause, but every librarian can aspire to the Indianapolis staff's absence of stuffiness, abundance of enthusiasm, and willingness to take risks in order to enrich the experiences of museum patrons by helping them "read more about it."

All departments and functions of the museum will find bibliographies useful, and individuals who use the collection to any extent will undoubtedly want to have materials located for them outside of the library. The well-selected bibliography introduces new materials to potential readership. For example, in the course of their work, the exhibits staff and the education departments may give such materials to visitors to take home as reminders of their museum experience and as links between the museum and their daily lives.

The membership and public relations offices use bibliographies in a similar manner—as an encouragement to renew membership, as an inducement to visit, as a boost to the credentials of an exhibit, and as a connection to other communication agencies in the community. Curators and exhibitors may issue a joint bibliography, while curation and registration, as departments and functions, find it useful to have on hand a list of references that explain what they do in the museum.

Planning for Services

Information services are the library's visible *raison d'être*, the above-ground flowering that flourishes from the roots of planning and technical services. The quality of the information service either discredits the library or enhances its credibility within the museum.

Planning and providing for information services involve several phases, which depend on the mission of the museum, the resources (both on hand and potential), and the skills and expertise of the library staff. Good planning depends on and emphasizes feedback and suggestions from those being served; surveys— both the formal, paper kind and the informal, water-cooler type; and self-study and self-evaluation on the part of library staff.[17]

The results of an information audit are invaluable in deciding what services to offer, both at the start, and later as the library grows and changes. The four services discussed in this chapter—circulation, reference, retrieval, and bibliographical—can be thought of as the core services most patrons will expect from a library. We shall look at extended services—the other six—in the next chapter.

In Summary

Information services entails a broad range of activities to be carried out by the museum library staff in support of the museum, its staff, and its patrons. In meeting the information needs of users, the library must make early decisions about service claims and priorities and establish policies on its reference and bibliographic services.

Starting-Up

The library starting from ground zero will necessarily be limited in the information services that can initially be offered. The staff can certainly from the beginning aim for *circulation* and *print-based reference* services for the museum staff.

1. The library staff in writing the collection development policy and in securing the opening-day collection emphasizes *reference materials*. Appropriate nonbook and nonprint reference resources should also be included in the initial collection: terrestrial globe and sky maps, taxonomic charts, art slides, local type collections, and so on.

2. The library staff establishes *policies* for circulation and reference, including the population to be served, the type of service, and the extent of resource seeking and sharing with other agencies. Plans should be made at this time for continuing surveys of user needs.

3. The staff also initially includes—if possible—basic bibliographic services such as *book verification and location*, and *retrieving articles* from magazines and journals. These services may either use in-house resources or be available by arrangement with cooperating libraries.

4. Meanwhile, the library staff makes plans to *add electronic retrieval* resources, both CD-ROM and online. They also inform the museum staff of such long-range plans, with the expectation that demand will hasten the day of the library's computerization. Thus they will be prepared to offer the service, if and when a computer is available—even if elsewhere in the museum and only at certain times.

5. After surveying the museum staff and studying their own interests and actual expertise—or the possibilities of developing expertise!—the library staff begins to add to its menu of information services, including those discussed in this chapter, and the extended services introduced in chapter 7.

Revitalizing

The library staff trying to begin again or to revitalize a faltering information service has, in some ways, the more difficult task. For one thing, the museum staff will either have become used to the present level of service and so resent changes in their habits, or—more likely—they will have given up on the library, by-passing it when seeking information. Hence, some marketing and public relations will be necessary while the preparations for service are underway.

1. With the collection development policy in hand, the library staff *evaluates the reference collection* and upgrades and replaces it, while at the same time looking for nonbook and nonprint materials to augment the collection. The initial emphasis will be on quick reference resources, periodical indexes, dictionaries and handbooks in the museum's subject field.

2. The library staff examines the recorded evidence in the library and queries the museum staff to determine what information services were *previously offered*, and which should be maintained, revised or added.

3. Based on these findings, the staff develops and publicizes the circulation and reference *policies*.

4. See step 3, above.

5. See step 4, above.

6. See step 5, above.

Notes

1. Virginia Boucher, *Interlibrary Loan Practices Handbook*, 2nd ed. (Chicago: ALA, 1997); and Leslie R. Morris, *Interlibrary Loan Policies Directory*, 6th. ed. (New York: Neal-Schuman, 1999).

2. Esther Green Bierbaum, "Museum Libraries: The More Things Change....," *Special Libraries* 87/2 (Spring, 1996), p. 82.

3. Email, where available, is another avenue of quick reference service, and a way to take the library to the library user; see Anne Grodzins Lipow, "'In Your Face Reference Service,'" *Library Journal* 124/13 (August 1999): 50–52.

4. Leonard Will, "Museums as Information Centres," *Museum International*, No. 181 46/1 (1996): 20–25.

5. The e-book is an emerging nonprint format that has reference potential. Some models hold 100,000 pages and are completely portable; content in most instances is downloaded from a proprietary source. See Judy Luther, "E-Books: The Next Electronic Frontier," *Information Today* 15/11 (December 1998): 32–34.

6. Elaine Zarenba Jennerich, *The Reference Interview As a Creative Art* (Littleton, Colo.: Libraries Unlimited, 1987.)

7. Will, "Museums," p. 23.

8. Wouter Van Gils, "The Paperless Library: Between Myth and Museum," *Information Services and Use* 14/1 (1994): 9–17.

9. For some direct and practical criteria for evaluating Web sites, *see*: Tina Kelley, "How to Separate Good Data From Bad," *The New York Times* (Thursday, 4 March 1999): D4.

10. See, for example Amerial Kassel, "Internet Power Searching: Finding Pearls in a Zillion Grains of Sand," *Information Outlook* 3/4 (April 1999): 28–32. The author includes a list of metadata sources.

11. Charles R. McClure, and Betsy Reifsnider, "Performance Measures for Corporate Information Centers," *Special Libraries* 74/3 (July 1983): 193–204.

12. Peter Hernon, and Charles R. McClure, "The 55 Percent Rule," *Library Journal* 111/7 (15 April 1986): 37–41. Studies of reference service based on unobtrusive observation as well as on factual tests have been criticized on methodological grounds. For a more extensive discussion of the issue, see Sharon L. Baker and F. Wilfrid Lancaster, *The Measurement and Evaluation of Library Services*, 2nd ed. (Arlington, Va.: Information Resources Press, 1991), pp. 246–256. Some studies do show that certain influential factors, such as familiarity with the collection, reference interview skills, and knowledge of the field, are all amenable to improvement through professional development and on-the-job guidance.

13. James A. Talaga, "Concept of Price in a Library Context," *Journal of Library Administration* 14/4 (1991): 87–101.

14. Hilda L. Jay, and M. Ellen Jay, *Developing Library-Museum Partnerships to Serve Young People* (Hamden, Conn.: Library Professional Publications, 1984), pp. 23–24.

15. Two standard manuals are *The Chicago Manual of Style*, 14th ed. (Chicago: University of Chicago Press, 1993); and Kate Turabian, *A Manual for Writers of Term Papers, Theses, and Dissertations*, 6th ed., rev. by John Grossman and Alice Bennett (Chicago: University of Chicago Press, 1996). Unless the museum's researchers and curators have made a prior decision to use other styles, the library staff may wish to adopt one of these manuals, which are familiar to readers and also are largely self-explanatory.

16. Nancy Cammack, "Rex's Lending Center Is a Roaring Success," *American Libraries* 24/5 (May 1993): 428–431.

17. While it is directed at academic librarians and their institutions, much of the following resource is also applicable to the museum library setting: Wanda K. Johnston, *Library and Learning Resource Programs: Evaluation and Self-Study* (Chicago: Association of College and Research Libraries/ALA, 1998).

Further Reading

Circulation

Boucher, Virginia. *Interlibrary Loan Practices Handbook*. 2nd ed. Chicago: ALA, 1997.

Ellison, John W., and Patricia Ann Coty, eds. *Nonbook Media: Collection Management and User Services*. Chicago: ALA, 1987.

Morris, Leslie R. *Interlibrary Loan Policies Directory*. 6th ed. New York: Neal-Schuman, 1999.

Smith, G. Guy. "A Lawyer's Perspective on Confidentiality." *American Libraries* 19/6 (June 1988): 453.

Wayne, K.M. "Access and Privacy: Ethics in Library, Archival and Visual Resource Collections." *Art Documentation* 10 (Summer 1991): 88–89.

Reference and Retrieval

Baker, Sharon L., and F. Wilfrid Lancaster. *The Measurement and Evaluation of Library Services*. 2nd ed. Arlington, Va.: Information Resources Press, 1991.

Berkman, Bob. *Find It Fast: How to Uncover Expert Information on Virtually Any Subject*. New York: Harcourt Brace World, 1987.

Gates, Jean Key. *Guide to the Use of Libraries and Information Sources*. 7th ed. New York: McGraw-Hill, 1994.

Hernon, Peter, and Charles R. McClure. "The 55 percent Rule." *Library Journal* 111/7 (15 April 1986): 37–41.

Jennerich, Elaine Zaremba. *The Reference Interview As a Creative Art*. Littleton, Colo.: Libraries Unlimited, 1987.

Katz, William A. *Introduction to Reference Work*. 7th ed. New York: McGraw-Hill, 1997.

McClure, Charles R., and Betsy Reifsnyder. "Performance Measures for Corporate Information Centers." *Special Libraries* 74/3 (July 1983): 193–204.

Richardson, John V., Jr. "Understanding the Reference Transaction: A Systems Analysis Perspective." *College and Research Libraries* 60/3 (May 1999): 211–222.

Stam, Deirdre C. "Tracking Art Historians: On Information Needs and Information-Seeking Behaviour." *Art Libraries* Journal 14/3 (1989): 13–16.

Bibliographic Services

Turabian, Kate L. *A Manual for Writers of Term Papers, Theses, and Dissertations*. 6th ed. rev., by John Grossman and Alice Bennett. Chicago: University of Chicago Press, 1996.

University of Chicago. *The Chicago Manual of Style*. 14th ed. Chicago: University of Chicago Press, 1993.

Chapter 7

Being Special: Extended Information Services

The *What* and the *Why* of Extended Services

Extended information services are the signature-pieces of the special library. Tailored to the needs of the library's patrons (in the museum, that includes all administrators, all staff, and all board members) these services place data and information in the hands or on the computer screens of those patrons.

Extended services are provided as much as sought; that is, if the library staff is really tuned in to the parent organization, the information arrives before the need is expressed. These services are challenging and sometimes stressful—but they are also opportunities for creatively making a difference within the organization.

Extended services raise the library's profile well above the patrons' horizons—a mixed blessing unless the library staff is prepared, because when the museum staff gets wind of the possibilities, extended services may be in greater demand than the reference and bibliographic services discussed in chapter 6. In fact, museum staff may ask for such extended services—by description, if not by name—ahead of some of the basic services.

Specialized Information Services

The two specialized services most frequently cited in the special libraries literature, and the two that can make the greatest impression on the library's patrons, are current awareness (CA) and selective dissemination of information (SDI).

Current awareness (CA). Current awareness provides generalized and up-to-date data and information in such areas as staff research, the museum's mission, museological developments, the museum's current and future exhibits, and business and administrative concerns. The assumption is that most people in the museum, docents included, will have at least a passing interest in the CA information.

There are various ways to organize a program of current awareness. The librarian may circulate the contents pages of journals among museum staff members, who then request from the library the journals containing the articles, or photocopies of the articles, in which they are interested. Some librarians clip articles from newspapers and popular magazines on topics of interest to museum staff, and then gather them into captioned folders or labeled notebooks. Folder or notebook is then routed to museum staff members or placed in a designated spot in the library for staff use. The staff lounge is another likely spot for such materials, which might include news of fund-raising projects, reviews of exhibits, or articles about the museum's subject field written for the general public—a good means of insight into the information level of the museum visitor.

Other current awareness strategies, depending upon the patrons being served, include both an up-date bulletin board (to which museum staff should also contribute) and a library newsnotes or report sheet, listing news, events and developments in the museum field in general and the museum's subject area in particular, grant and funding opportunities, and calls for papers.

When the museum has email, whether through the Internet, or locally, by LAN or intranet, the library staff is readily able to pop the CA content onto the screens of staff members, using a group mailing list. Staff members like this method because they can pick and choose what to download. One caution, however: beware of sending too much content in a CA dispatch; overloading the system or the recipients is not conducive to sunny public relations.

The primary purpose and viewpoint of the current awareness service is to collect recent data and information of general interest to the organization's staff, and to distribute the materials as quickly and conveniently as possible. Much of the information included in current awareness comes automatically to the librarian's hand in the course of dealing with the day's mail. The service—and the consequent cost in time and effort—consists of assembling the informational items and devising a system that ensures that everyone receives the package.

Selective dissemination of information (SDI). This service may sound like a faintly medical solution to the information needs of professionals practicing within an organization. More specific and personalized than current awareness, it is based upon the research, subject orientation, and professional development information requirements of a museum administrator or staff member, or of a small group of individuals engaged in the same research, project, or activity.

As the term implies, the data are carefully chosen for and delivered to the person in question. Material gathered for an SDI request is not circulated, nor does the librarian reveal its content to others. SDI begins with a needs profile for a particular museum staff person. For example, a curator developing the documentation for a type of furniture manufactured in the region may need confirmation about secondary woods or hardware designers. The librarian prepares a data sheet under the curator's name, and together they decide on likely data sources: journals the curator does not usually read, local interest sections in regional and specialty magazines, advertising from back issues of newspapers and magazines, forestry and lumber reports, and information from the archives of furniture manufacturers and retailers. Archival sources are searched systematically and checked off; current sources are checked as published. When the means are there, much SDI information can also be delivered electronically, including the contents pages of journals of particular interest.[1]

Obviously, SDI programs, even more than current awareness programs, require investments of time and other resources on the part of the librarian and library staff. CA reports, once the data are assembled, can be reproduced and routed by library assistants, whether salaried or volunteer. Library staff may also be involved in gathering data, and knowledgeable volunteers make excellent newspaper and magazine clippers. However, SDI usually requires a more rigorous approach to sources, a more detailed knowledge of the field of investigation, and a greater facility in the use of print and database sources.

Even so, library staff can often handle the searching of specific current sources, and volunteers may have backgrounds, or can be trained, in archival methods. If staff other than the librarian are involved in SDI projects, they must appreciate that the relationship is one of privilege, that privacy and confidentiality are aspects of the SDI service.

Specialized information services are valuable to museum staff members as a way to increase their knowledge and extend their research reach. In the beginning, however, there may be resistance. Professionals trust primarily their own data-collecting efforts, and most have not learned in the course of their training to ask for information guidance. In overcoming initial resistance, one librarian's strategy has been to inquire about a current project and then to supply some pertinent data with a "hope this helps" memo. If the information is useful, the word will spread.

Sometimes the word spreads to such an extent that these services consume a large chunk of library resources—not an unhappy problem, but one requiring negotiation. The wise librarian will have anticipated such a predicament and written service priorities into library policy. The librarian can also make an estimate of future demands on library staff by keeping track of the volume of response to the service.

Other staff members for whom SDI is valuable are in the membership office and the grant-writing programs, where local news and national trends are matters of interest. Members of the board, particularly the new members, are also SDI targets. In some museums, new board members are given an information packet containing a history of the museum, its mission and goals, descriptions of its subject area or areas, highlights of functions and departments, and profiles of its members and the community it serves. Volunteers such as docents and library assistants also find such a packet useful.

A note regarding copyright. Because data and information retrieval and the specialized information services of CA and SDI involve copying and distributing copyrighted text, the librarian should be aware of the Copyright Act of 1976 and its revisions, and be prepared to observe its provisions.[2] The librarian must be ready to be the copyright watchdog, interpreter, and instructor for patrons and museum staff.

Because museums are nonprofit and educational, they reap the benefits of *fair use* and other concessions of the law. Fair use itself is coming under siege, however, and even for the not-for-profit organization, it is better to err on the side of strict interpretation than to risk a questionable practice or an unethical stance in regard to the law.

Thus, in providing information services, care should be taken to acknowledge and cite all sources and to limit photocopying or mechanical copying. To make library users aware of copyright limitations, the librarians should post a copyright notice next to each copy machine and have fliers on the law to hand out.

Information regarding software and online resources should be included in the flier and next to computer terminals. Since software is intellectual content in the same sense as words on the page of a journal, the library must be the role model in observing licensing agreements, copying restrictions, and limitations on access. The public understands copyright in regard to second editions of books; software upgrades are analogous purchases, not to be pirated.

Data Analysis

Data analysis and the creation of information are other service areas in which special librarians are increasingly engaged. As we have noted, the library's reference service points to sources of data or locates and reports the data as found, and while librarians have standards for evaluating reference sources, in providing reference service they do not weigh the contents, except in instances of egregious error or evident bias on the part of the author.

Special librarians are now being called upon to direct their bibliographic expertise and subject knowledge to assembling, analyzing, and evaluating data and in so doing, to create new information rather than providing reference services alone.[3] Data analysis is relatively new territory for librarians, yet it is a natural outgrowth of the data gathering and evaluating already conducted for CA and SDI services. Julia Matthews, for example, reports success in providing senior managers at the Royal Ontario Museum (ROM) with an information packet on mission and planning.[4]

This type of information service can also be brought to bear on *management information systems* (MIS), the compilation and packaging of data generated by and about the museum or other organization.[5] The added dimension is the analyzing and recasting of data and the creating of an information document—a paper, a report, or a datadisk. The production of such documents is an aspect of the professional partnership enjoyed by many special librarians who have carefully and creatively directed the library services toward the support of the parent organization. Spreadsheet and graphics software allow data to be presented in colorful and meaningful ways.

Desktop publishing software has helped make the creation and production of documents relatively painless and also widespread. The librarian who becomes a document producer as part of the library's information services should take the time to learn some basic principles of typography and page make-up and design to avoid the clutter and glitz—"chart junk"[6]—that tend to be the thumbprint of the amateur. (The mark of the amateur has been imprinted on many Web pages as well.) Desktop software manuals are often helpful. The librarian needs also to become a student of other's brochures and reports, analyzing what works and what does not. Skills in page design and document creation are readily transferred to the library's annual reports, newsletters, and other communications.

Overall, the museum administration and board are more likely to ask the librarian for data analysis than the museum staff, because professional staff feel a professional responsibility for their own data analysis, and the creation of information is part of their scholarly calling. But in many administrative planning situations, data alone are insufficient to the needs of the group. For example, the museum board planning a building campaign will need a complex package of data on local economics, projections for future growth, school curricula, present demographics and future projections, and the success of building-fund campaigns undertaken by similar museums. These data, retrieved from many sources, are not likely to have much significance until expressed as information about local fund-raising and the likelihood for success. The museum librarian who has actively represented the library in meetings and who is known for assembling correct and pertinent data is more likely to receive this sort of information-analysis assignment.

The business and membership offices needing information about trends in not-for-profit organizations, the influence of tax legislation, changes in the economic and demographic structure of the community, and research on programs and costs are also likely to call on the library staff for data analysis.

Bibliographic and User Instruction

Special librarians are recapturing the traditional roles of scholar and teacher in the gathering and analysis of data and in teaching bibliographic techniques and the use of databases.[7] Bibliographic instruction can range, according to the need of the patron, from instruction about the catalog and explanations about the headings and the content of the records to extended series of classes in library research methods, multimedia resources, and bibliographic citation. Museums that conduct laboratory or research classes for youth call on the librarian for instruction in bibliographic searches, especially in the journal literature, and for guidance in creating notes and citations.

"End-user," in library-speak, generally refers to a nonlibrarian using bibliographic utilities and other databases to search for bibliographic resources—that is, the library patron looking for a monograph on OCLC or a dataset of journal articles on ERIC. To some librarians the end-user has become a philosophical as well as information service issue: can the librarian abrogate a professional activity to the lay person?

Two issues are actually involved here: the librarian's inner vision of his or her role, and the library's satisfactory fulfillment of the patron's information needs. If the librarian feels deeply that database searching in part defines his or her professional role, then end-user instruction will not be a comfortable and natural part of the library's instructional goals. If the librarian perceives the database as just another data source, the use of which can be taught as the use of *Biological Abstracts* can be taught, then the question becomes the degree of thoroughness and value the end-user is able to achieve.

Until the end-user becomes as proficient as the librarian, a good compromise is to have the patron conduct a preliminary and exploratory search, with the understanding that the librarian will, if asked, try other approaches in order to recover other data. Economics may force the issue when the business office requires the library to conduct the quickest, shortest, and most efficient searches, no matter who poses the search request.

The Internet has added a new dimension to the end-user issue. In one sense, it has made everyone an end-user. However, unlike proprietary and governmental online databases, very little on the Internet can be taken at face value, and some of the sources are worth exactly what the searcher pays for them: nothing. The librarian's instructional role becomes that of evaluating guide rather than finding facilitator.

All museum personnel stand to benefit from bibliographic instruction, some more than others. Museum members and individuals enrolled in educational programs are the groups most amenable to class formats. Others may prefer individual instruction on an as-needed basis.

Programs, Exhibits and Outreach

To the extent staff and resources permit, the library should cooperate with the exhibit and education departments by publicizing, reinforcing, and supplementing their efforts. Obviously, the librarian needs to be aware of present and future plans in those departments not only because those plans will affect the collection and information services, but also because of what the library can contribute to the public's knowledge and understanding of the museum's work.

Library programming can take various directions: book talks, book reviews, and introduction of materials on a special topic to various audiences; library-prepared materials on a topic, accompanied by talks and lectures, or slide or videotape productions; exhibits of relevant library materials or of excerpts from the main exhibit; and off-site presentations, either alone or in support of museum outreach. As suggested in chapter 5, participation in community-wide programs is another way the museum library can offer a visible service and also enhance its parent organization.[8] For example, the librarian of the Cleveland Museum of Natural History logs in as "Dr. Dino" on the city's Free-Net, an open-access computer system, to answer science reference questions.[9] Enthusiasm and an understanding of the audience are of higher priority for such undertakings than a dinosaur costume.

The service potential of library programming and exhibits, whether on-site or outreach, is unlimited. The library can—and should—be a public relations force in the same manner as education, curation, or the speaker's bureau. Indeed, because of their information and communication skills, librarians are often included in the speaker's bureau roster.

Careful strategic planning should precede any programming undertakings. Results can be unexpected, particularly when successful library programs and exhibits come up short of support and resources. Here, again, the library's goals and published policies can help the staff establish bounds and guidelines for accepting or instituting programming assignments.

Conservation and Preservation

The library staff is responsible for caring for the collection, maintaining the items in usable form, and keeping them for future use. Sometimes these goals require intervention strategies ranging from simple repairs, through rebinding, to a reconstruction of the book or object.

As noted in chapter 2, the terms, conservation and preservation, are often used interchangeably, or as a pair with equal weight, such as black and white. When distinctions are made, conservation is the broader of the two, subsuming preservation and referring to "the efforts needed to ensure that the historical and material evidence of the object is not diminished."[10]

The best conservation techniques are considered to be those which are reversible. In the case of books and documents, as much as feasible of the original physical entity is retained. Preservation includes techniques of substituting one form for another and transforming damaged materials into usable formats, such as photocopying damaged pages or converting a fragile document to microfilm.

Museums, of course, invest large chunks of their resources in the conservation and preservation of the objects in the collections. Curators and interpreters are forthright in identifying as replicas objects that have been created for use in exhibits or programs to preserve the originals; they restore objects to what their scholarly research suggests was an original condition; and they employ a wide range of conservation techniques to control deterioration and provide suitable environmental conditions. Museum librarians who have such conservatorial resources at hand are able to care for their own collections in exemplary style. In museums with inadequate resources for conservation, librarians may be required to care for the materials on their own, at least to the extent of providing information about the best practices.

Museums, archives and libraries share a major concern about the acidification of paper, a condition which has resulted in the crumbling into dust of much of the written record of the past 100 years. The development of cheaper, woodpulp paper and the advent of high-speed printing inks, plus the use of new chemical bonds and paper bindings was a two-edged sword: it had the salutary effect of making books less expensive and more widely available—helping to make possible the great public library movement of the turn of the century—but it also carried the built-in seeds of self-destruction as the new chemicals in paper, ink, and bindings all reacted together to form book-eating acids. In purchasing new library materials, librarians now look for the infinity symbol [∞] of acid-free paper; but they must still contend with the forces silently eating away at a century's worth of their collections.[11]

Paper is not the only information-bearing substance that is going the way of dust and deterioration. Other materials and formats are being ravaged by the march of technology as much as by time. As one technology wins public favor, another goes into oblivion. (Witness Beta, lost to VHS; vinyl records scrapped for the CD-ROM!) Electronic media are also notoriously unstable. (Watch that magnetic screwdriver!)

In the case of computers, the machines—the hardware—that accept the tapes or disks change operating systems, architecture, and software, seemingly month by month. The National Archives, for example, keeps a "museum" of various machines.[12] Probably the more significant problem is software obsolescence.[13]

Migration—translating the electronic information from one storage medium to another—is only a partial solution because the procedure is time-consuming and expensive, and because data are lost in the migration.[14] The museum library that expects to collect electronic media needs to decide on the conservation measures it will undertake, if any, and to include them in the collection management documents.

The library's conservation and preservation responsibilities will depend upon the museum's conservation program and policies as a whole and the library's assigned and assumed participation. These responsibilities can range from providing current materials in the theory and practice of conservation and preservation, and locating technical data relevant to preservation, through to assisting or collaborating in the program, or even managing paper and nonprint media preservation as part of the library's collection management. Certainly the librarian or a staff member will need to keep up with the changes in the field and be able to offer consultation and advice.

All members of the museum community will benefit from efforts to keep the human record readable, visible, or audible; turf is not a consideration except, perhaps, when costs and resources are allocated.

Archival Services

Libraries and museums are enthusiastic gatherers of the archives of other organizations but do less well in regard to their own.[15] Museums usually have two universes of archives: those pertaining to the subject area (as in a history museum), which are subject to the same curatorial care as the objects; and those pertaining to the life and history of the museum itself, which may be scattered in various offices, housed in the garages of successive board presidents, or otherwise subject to no particular care at all. The library staff that adopts the museum's internal archives does its parent organization an enduring favor.

Museum archives of both sorts require both conservation *and* preservation. A common strategy is to place the original documents in safe-keeping elsewhere and to use photocopies in the active historical files. If the materials are not often consulted, photoreduction techniques, such as microfilm and microfiche, preserve the encoded message, leaving the originals for occasional reference or scholarly examination. Scholars respect the need for care of the original documents but also feel they learn much from the original—from the paper and the way it was folded, the ink blots and misstrokes of the pen, and the color of ink and paper—which is beyond the reproductive power of the microfilming camera.

The storage of archives is of particular importance. The environment must be free from dust, rust, insects, excessive moisture and light, and access to the materials must be controlled. The storage of other materials is also a conservation consideration: nonmagnetic and dust-free environments should be maintained for electronic data and audiotapes, cool temperatures for audiodiscs and film, and acid-free storage for graphic materials.

Conservation and preservation procedures are crucial in archives management. Special libraries associated with a conservation-oriented parent organization have emphasized this aspect of collection management, and many special librarians are also members of the Society of American Archivists (SAA) or follow the work of that association closely. The contributions of SAA include a series of technical manuals for various formats and collections.[16] This aspect of archives includes the evaluation of documents, and participating in the museum's security and catastrophe programs to ensure that archives and documents are given high priority for safe handling, secure use and storage, and disaster management.

However, mere keeping is no more the whole of archives than is shelving the whole of library collections; knowledge of the content and access to it are also necessary. For these tasks, the library provides a catalog, and the archive develops finding aids and indexes, which, in the paper-based environment, are folders and cards.

Archival principles operate at the collection level, rather than the library's individual item level, a difference that was overlooked in the early development of AACR. Addressing this issue, Archives, Personal Papers and Manuscripts (APPM), as a format, was based on both ISBD and archives practice. More recently, electronic methodologies have brought the library and archival worlds closer together with the MARC-AMC format (now to be integrated into MARC 21). Hence the library is the logical repository of the metadata—data about data—for both the library collection and the library or museum archives.

In Summary

Specialized, extended information services can increase the knowledge base of museum staff members, extending their research reach and widening and deepening the aesthetic and learning experiences of the museum visitor. They also make the library more than a handy spot for books and journals, although a carefully selected and developed collection (and the catalog that unlocks it) is the foundation for effective and efficient information services.

Those services beyond circulation procedures and the provision of reference resources and quick reference services, are in the hands of the librarian and library staff; neither consultants nor volunteers can sustain the planning, oversight, and evaluation necessary to administer an active program of extended information services. Moreover, the librarian must be knowledgeable about the museum, its staff, collections, and programs and should take an active, visible part in the internal affairs of the museum.

Consequently, the planning steps for extended services come down to a series of decision points, both for the starting-up library and the library working on revitalization.

Starting Up and Revitalizing

1. *Choosing the services.* Near-infinite variations and combinations of information services exist, and no two museum libraries are alike in what they offer and to whom. Beyond the basics of circulation and provision of reference sources, the librarian must select a few services that the collection and staff can support and which most closely reflect the museum's mission. (Data retrieval will probably be one and bibliographic services, another.)

   Planning to provide those services should include staff training, schedule changes, if necessary, and the writing of service policies and procedures. This latter information should be included in an announcement circulated to all museum staff, along with examples of data retrieval and bibliographies.

2. *Promoting the services.* As a student of the organization, the librarian should learn about proposed projects and grant applications, new accessions and exhibits, and plans for new educational programming. Here, again, an information audit would be appropriate and helpful.

   The librarian truly sensitive to the information needs of the museum staff can respond in advance of an expressed need. Indeed, the dilemma such a librarian faces becomes one of balancing the demands of information services against the library's materials acquisition and organization functions, which must continue in order to have an information service at all. A motto here: "*Always promote; and always deliver.*" (See also chapter 5, p. 86, "Marketing the Library.")

3. *Widening the reach of services.* When the information needs of administration and staff are well served, the librarian looks to museum members, visitors, and the general public—probably in that order—as information services clients. Services to the museum's members and to the public include data retrieval and telephone reference, exhibits, bibliographies, and book talks—all activities that also promote the role of the museum in the community. While the cost of information services can be shown to be less than the value of the public relations the services engender, it is up to the librarian to conduct the research.

4. *Measuring and Evaluating the Services.* A program for measuring and evaluating information services is as essential as the services themselves, not only to show the value of the services in terms of public relations, but to help the library staff shape the services to meet the museum's needs. If the librarian cannot be certain that the needs of the museum library's clientele are being met (within, of course, the mission guidelines of the museum and the policies of the library), one of two things will happen: resources will be wasted or information needs will be unmet.

   A mix of techniques provides the most rounded picture. Among them are surveys of library users and non-users; statistical records, such as questions answered, documents retrieved, SDIs prepared; and unobtrusive observation.[17] With data results from such research, the library staff can safely drop an underused service or expand one in high demand.

Notes

1. G. Lynn Tinsley, "An Electronic Bulletin Board," *Special Libraries* 80/3 (Summer 1989): 188–192.

2. For information regarding copyright in libraries and educational settings, see Laura N. Gasaway and Susan K. Wiant, *Libraries and Copyright: A Guide to Copyright Law in the 1990s* (Washington, D.C.: Special Libraries Association, 1994); for guidance on copyright applied to museum and library documents, see Stephen E. Weil, "Copyrights and Wrongs," *Museum News* 72/4 (July-August 1993): 40–43, 63. Meanwhile, technology has gotten ahead of the law; the Internet has introduced new ways to exploit and also to violate copyright. There are many gray areas in which case law is still being developed, but the library literature carries articles about electronic publications and

copyright issues. See, for example, Janet Balas, "Copyright in the Digital Era," *Computers in Libraries*, 18/6 (June 1998): 38–40. See also the copyright section of "Further Reading."

3. The library literature is actively recognizing these new roles. See, for example, Stuart Basefsky, "The Library as Agent of Change: Pushing the Client Institution Forward," *Information Outlook* 3/8 (August 1999): 37–40, describing the functions of several roles; and "The Librarian as Editor," *The One-Person Library* 3/10 (February 1987): 1-3, delineating a particular one.

4. Julia Matthews, "From Archaeology to Zoology: the ROM Library," *Canadian Library Journal* 43/3 (June 1986): 187–190.

5. For a classic, general treatment of the nature and function of management information systems (MIS), see Rolland Hurtubise, *Management Information Systems: Concepts and Tools* (West Hartford, Conn.: Kumarian Press, 1984). For more recent information, see Kenneth A. Megill, *The Corporate Memory: Information Management in the Electronic Age* (London: BowkerSaur, 1997).

6. Edward R. Tufte, *The Visual Display of Quantitative Information* (Cheshire, Conn.: Graphics Press, 1990), pp. 108–121.

7. For an overview of some of the issues of library user instruction, particularly in the not-for-profit sector, see Martha Jane K. Zachert, *Educational Services in Special Libraries: Planning and Administration* (Chicago: Medical Library Association, 1990).

8. For many suggestions applicable to both the museum and the library in the museum, see Hilda L. Jay, and M. Ellen Jay, *Developing Library-Museum Partnerships to Serve Young People* (Hamden, Conn.: Library Professional Publications, 1984).

9. Nancy Cammack, "Rex's Lending Center Is a Roaring Success," *American Libraries* 24/5 (May 1993): 428–431.

10. John M. A. Thompson, ed., *Manual of Curatorship: A Guide to Museum Practice* (London: Butterworths, 1984), p. 277.

11. *Slow Fires: On the Preservation of the Human Record*, sponsored by the Council on Library Resources, the Library of Congress, and the National Endowment for the Humanities (Santa Monica, Calif.: American Film Foundation, 1987). Video.

12. John W. Carlin, "Your Past Is Disappearing: What Museums Should Know About the 20th-Century Archives Crisis," *Museum News* 78/1 (January/February 1999): 46–49.

13. Margaret Hedstrom, "Electronic Records Research: What Have Archivists Learned from Mistakes of the Past?" *Archives and Museum Informatics* 10/4 (1996): 313–325.

14. Katie Hafner, "Books to Bytes: The Electronic Archive," *The New York Times* 8 April 1999), D1.

15. Patrick J. Boylan, "Museum and Archives in the Contemporary World," *International Review on Archives* [XXX] 30 (1984): 39–52; p. 48.

16. For information about the programs and publications of the Society of American Archivists, consult the Society's Web page at http://www.archivists.org.

17. For a thorough treatment of the subject, see Sharon L. Baker and F. Wilfrid Lancaster, *Measurement and Evaluation and Evaluation of Library Services*, 2nd ed. (Arlington, Va.: Information Resources, 1991).

Further Reading

Copyright

Bielefield, Arlene, and Lawrence Cheeseman. *Libraries and Copyright Law*. New York: Neal-Schuman, 1993.

"Copyright and Fair Use." Palo Alto, Calif.: Stanford University Libraries; Council on Library and Information Resources, no update given: http://fairuse.stanford.edu (accessed August 2000).

Copyright Clearance Center. "Copyright and Photocopy Permissions Questions and Answers." Available by mail from CCC, 222 Rosewood Drive, Danvers, MA 01923. Full information, including the text of the law, available at http://www.copyright.com (accessed August 2000).

Liblicense: A Resource for Librarians. New Haven: Yale University Library; Council on Library and Information Resources, updated 30 May 2000: http://www.library.yale.edu/~llicense/index.shtml (accessed August 2000).

McDonald, Steven. "The Laws of Cyberspace: What Colleges Need to Know." *The Chronicle of Higher Education* (31 October 1997): A68.

Okerson, Ann. "Who Owns Digital Works?" *Scientific American* 278/1 (July 1996): 80–84. Also online at www.sciam.com/0796issue/0796okerson.html (accessed August 2000).

Reed, Mary Hutchinson. *The Copyright Primer for Librarians and Educators*. Chicago: ALA, 1987.

United States Copyright Office. Available at http://lcweb.loc.gov/copyright (updated 15 August 2000; accessed August 2000).

Extended Information Services

Basefsky, Stuart. "The Library As an Agent of Change: Pushing the Client Institution Forward." *Information Outlook* 3/8 (August 1999): 37–40.

Bell, Hope A. "The Librarian As Trainer." *Information Outlook* 2/4 (April 1998): 17–20.

Tufte, Edward R. *Envisioning Information*. Cheshire, Conn.: Graphics Press, 1990.

_____. *The Visual Display of Quantitative Information*. Cheshire, Conn.: Graphics Press, 1983.

_____. *Visual Explanations: Images and Quantities, Evidence and Narrative*. Cheshire, Conn.: Graphics Press, 1997.

Zachert, Martha Jane K. *Educational Services in Special Libraries: Planning and Administration*. Chicago: Medical Library Association, 1990.

Conservation, Preservation, and Archives

[See also "Further Reading," chapter 2.]

Carlin, John W. "Your Past Is Disappearing: What Museums Should Know about the 20th-Century Archives Crisis." *Museum News* 78/1 (January/February 1999): 46–49.

Georgia Department of Archives and History. "Disaster Preparedness"; "Salvaging Your Valuable Personal Belongings." Available at http://www.sos.state.ga.us/archives/ps/gps.htm (accessed August 2000).

Chapter 8

Bits & Bytes:
Technology in the Library

A mystique continues to surround technology, especially the high technology of computers and other electronic devices. But technology is merely a tool, a method or process for handling a task, and the means of making human labor easier and more effective.

Technology offers the librarian many possibilities for reducing the volume of hands-on, manual procedures such as producing catalog cards from copy, creating written instructions for assistants, and recording the circulation of library materials. And, while *technology* popularly translates into "computers" and "automation," there are other means and strategies for reducing the burden of repetitious operations in the museum library. This chapter will first discuss low tech tools and then will look at the higher, or computerized, versions.

Mechanical and Traditional Aids

Mechanical and traditional aids tend to get overlooked in the rush to plug into electrical and electronic bells and whistles. But plugging-in can take time—often more time than manually executing the task. (Compare, for example, flipping the cards in an address file to accessing one's address file on a computer and then locating the particular name and address.) And for the paper-based library, alternatives to plugs and wires are a necessity. The following suggestions can simplify procedures, speed them up, or make them more accurate, all for a relatively small investment. Many other suggestions may be found in library supply catalogs.

Prepared forms. These might be perceived as a complete capitulation to the paper environment, except for the small library where paper *is* the environment. In these libraries, documents preprinted for specific purposes can save time and reduce errors. Cards for confirming appointments, or making bibliographic inquiries, or reporting data, or instructing library assistants in marking, filing, and shelving—all these forms provide a **written record**, a documentary memory base. In addition, preprinted routing slips for journals and cover memos for SDI are handy library tools. Prepared labels, particularly the self-adhesive variety, are also useful for denoting return addresses, temporary shelving locations, special instructions, and so on. Supply-house catalogs illustrate some of the variety available.

Copying and reproduction techniques. Preprinted forms suggest the technology for creating them—mimeograph, offset, and photocopy as well as letterpress. As noted in chapter 3, photocopy techniques may be used to speed catalog card production. Embossing printers, similar to the familiar charge plate machines, may be used with membership cards for circulation, reservations, and mail notices.

If a brief message is written more than twice a day, a rubber stamp can be used in place of preprinted forms. While it is all too easy to become stamp-happy, it is also simpler to stamp rather than type or write a message such as "Title requested is located in _____ room, _____ floor."

Card sorter. The sorter is a long, narrow stiff board, to which are attached alphabetized hinged flaps behind which the cards are slipped. If more than a dozen or so cards are to be filed at one time, this ancient and effective device helps the library staff not only sort the cards alphabetically but also store them in correct order until filing is completed. While designed principally for alphabetizing catalog cards, the device is also useful in organizing other kinds of materials and documents, such as pamphlets for the vertical file.

Photography. Cameras and photographic gear and processing tend to be ubiquitous in science and natural history museums and are popular in history and cultural museums. Thus the means and knowledge are at hand to record and preserve the library's records, or its more fragile materials, or to enlarge text or illustrations. Photographs of examples of shelf-ready books, journals tied for binding, or the results of other library procedures are useful and graphic additions to the staff handbook. Photographs of library furnishings, equipment, or three-dimensional objects are often required for inventory and insurance purposes, and may be used as well in reports, displays, and other publicity. When the time comes, digitized photographs can migrate to a Web site.

Typewriter. Clunky as it may be, there is still something to be said for the standard typewriter, including the fact that it is low-maintenance, self-explanatory in operation, more legible than most handwriting, and enables one to address an envelope or zip off a memo by the simple action of rolling in an envelope or scrap of paper and hitting the appropriate keys. While not the device of choice for creating sets of catalog cards, the typewriter can be used to make the master card that is to be replicated.

For many library tasks, then, the mechanical typewriter need not be held in scorn.

Electric Devices

Electricity was once the apex of technology and many electrical devices are still useful in the library.

Electric eraser. When data on bibliographic records must be changed, a good electric eraser can remove the text to be revised, thus sparing the staff the chore of retyping the entire card. The eraser is also useful for small housekeeping chores such as removing the library's ownership stamp from withdrawn items, cleaning the tops of books, and correcting slips of the marking pen. Some libraries also erase circulation records. Usually the motor-housing of the eraser fits comfortably in the hand, and the spindle to which the eraser head is attached is activated by turning the device in eraser-down position. Some models have off-on switches; the more expensive have a variable motor.

Electric pencil sharpener. Often overlooked, but a necessity in historical collections and archives where pens are proscribed, the electric pencil sharpener is far better than the mechanical grinder model for quiet operation, portability, and attractive design.

Heat pens and laminating irons. Unless the book vendor supplies cards and labels, inscribing or otherwise marking the call number on the book spine is an in-house project. A browse through a supply catalog suggests several means of accomplishing the task; self-adhering labels—written or typed—and heat- or transfer-embossing seem to be the most popular. Self-sticking labels are easy to read when typed with a primary font, while permanent ink should be used for hand-lettering. The adhesiveness of the labels can be enhanced with a strip of clear tape.

Unlike labels which present entanglement as the principal hazard, the heat pen is potentially dangerous and requires a considerable degree of skill, which is why pen and transfer tape have been largely superseded by label systems. The heat pen and transfer tape system is sometimes the best solution for marking surfaces to which even laminating tape does not adhere readily, and some labels still require heat application from a sealing iron. Encouraged to inquire, observe, and experiment, library assistants can evaluate the label options and recommend one or two methods, which may then be included in the staff manual.

Electric typewriter. The electric typewriter incorporates the advantages of the mechanical typewriter but is also much less tiring to use. When fitted with correcting tape and adjustable strike, it is indeed a boon to the organization operating in a paper environment and dependent to a great extent upon the services of volunteers. The variable strike means that multiple forms, no-carbon carbons, cards, and other heavy-duty materials may be safely accommodated. If it is to be used to create catalog cards, a card holder should be substituted for the regular paper guides; otherwise bent and torn cards are a frequent and frustrating occurrence.

Electronic Devices and Machines

Electric equipment uses electric current to power its operations; electronic equipment depends in addition upon the actions of electrons activated by electricity. The layperson's generalized distinction between electric and electronic—and the one assumed in this book—is based on the aspect of memory associated with the latter and on the equipment's response to an operator's actions. Thus the operator of an electric typewriter types, and printing results from the electrically powered key-striking action. The typing action can also be mechanically altered so that the operator can type back over errors with correcting tape. The electronic typewriter, in contrast, may be programmed (that is, directed or instructed) to hold a line or more of characters so that the operator can erase or alter portions of it; the printing takes place only after the operator makes the changes and takes a nontyping action such as pressing the PRINT key.

Electronic (memory) typewriter. The memory typewriter occupies a technological niche somewhat above the electric typewriter but below the personal computer (PC). (Memory means that, once a short document—such as a bibliographic record—is created, that document can be stored and replicated as many times as necessary. While the OFF switch usually erases the document, some memory typewriters also have a small amount of storage capacity on disk or tape so that the document can be recalled later rather than being lost.)

Equipped with memory, whether for one line or a short document, the electronic typewriter is a large step in the direction of higher technology and automation, while still handily accommodating the paper environment. It is a viable and relatively inexpensive solution for the museum library that produces records for the card catalog, either as original cataloging or from cataloging copy. In addition, the memory feature enables the library to produce and replicate various forms and documents.

Computers. As the selection of typewriters becomes narrower, and as the prices of desktop computers fall into the affordable range, many more museum libraries are taking the computerized plunge. One can perform many otherwise difficult tasks with ease on a PC; one cannot, however, spin in a piece of paper or an envelope and type a memo or address.

Computers come in many configurations, with varying amounts of memory and degrees of computing capacity. Printers are also endlessly varied. For the library just embarking on a computer project, it is well worth the small fee to have a reliable consultant evaluate its particular situation and needs to determine which two or three makes and models of machines and printers are most appropriate. This proviso suggests also that gift computers, which are likely to be graciously donated discards, will prove to be snares, delusions, and sources of frustration and discouragement.

No matter the size or configuration, all computers require instructions; they do not perform tasks by themselves. Of course, when prompted to do so, computers match and count with greater speed and accuracy than humans. Moreover, they do not tire, develop headaches, or need coffee breaks. But they also have bugs, can be infected by viruses, and go down at inopportune times.

For the librarian in the small museum, computerization may seem as remote and unlikely as a visit to the Ross Ice Shelf. However, since the mid–1980s, the desktop, or personal computer (the PC was once known as the microcomputer to distinguish it from the minicomputer, smaller range of mainframe) has steadily found its way into museum business offices. There it prints membership welcoming letters and mailing lists, stores the data for administrative annual reports that display pie charts and graphs, and projects expenses and budgets for the accounting department.[1]

In 1989 Richard Buchen reported his survey of museums and historical societies, finding that almost half of the museums he surveyed were using some level of computerization in collection management. He also noted that only 27 percent "had their book collections (at least in part) on computer," although he did not specify whether the book collection was regarded as a library.[2]

Ten years later, I found that in the museums surveyed, 93 percent of the business offices, 75 percent of the membership services, 68 percent of curators and registrars, and 61 percent of education departments used computers. At the same time in the same museums, 24 percent of the libraries had some level of computerization in their catalogs.

Data such as these indicate that the parent organizations of museum libraries have considerably increased the use of computers, while—for whatever reasons—the libraries have not. Still, the better news is that computers are there in museums, and that museum librarians should be able to secure some level of access to a PC, even when the library itself is not yet automated. The findings also mean that library computerization must be part of the librarian's long-range thinking and planning.

To understand better the types and uses of computer systems in libraries, we shall first look at computerized technology, or automation, in general terms and its development in libraries and museums.

Automation. Automation is the application of machines—particularly electronic machines—to particular tasks. Because computer applications often appear to the uninitiated to be self-regulated and self-operated, the term is popularly limited to operations controlled by computer. Many a siren song has been sung to the tune of automation, and many an organization, to achieve an automated state of grace, has purchased equipment beyond its needs and capacities or with unreasonably high expectations.

The ultimate purpose of computerized, automated processes is the same as for any technology: to relieve people of routine and repetitious manual tasks, which can be performed better some other way. People can then undertake human level (which is to say, *higher* level) activities such as planning user instruction, weeding the collection, or preparing a bibliography for the new color photography workshop.

The first and basic question to consider before adopting any technology is, "Do we need it?" Not all operations or organizations need to be automated. A small-scale, paper-based system which is unlikely to undergo growth in the near future—circulation in a staff-only museum library, for example—is not a prime candidate for technology. On the other hand, the library might give a high priority to transferring the regional historical society's index of county newspapers to an automated environment if the index is already successful as a paper system. Software suitable for smaller libraries often comes as a set of modules that control different functions and operations—cataloging, for example, or serials control—so that the librarian can automate selectively.

Experience and research have helped librarians discover some truths about what automation *will not* do:

- It will not save money, although it may permit resources to be redirected

- It will not salvage a non-functional paper system

- It will not produce gloriously formatted reports and records at the touch of a key

- It will not be self-explanatory and certainly will not eliminate the need for patron instruction in catalog use

On the other hand:

- It will require an enormous investment in planning, time, and effort
- It will, if well-planned, reduce laborious and tedious manual operations
- It will perform routine counting and matching operations faster and more accurately than humans
- It will, as an operation, very likely be perceived as more professional by those outside the library[3]

Computers in Libraries

The computer has become indispensable in many libraries for two different purposes: first, the creation and manipulation of data in-house, including the OPAC; second, the retrieval of data from distant sources through online searches. With the advent of specialized data management software for PCs, the two uses are merging.

Computerization began with boxes of punched cards fed in batches into a card reader (hence the term "batch mode," for bunched-up operations). The card reader transferred the bits (binary digits, which make up characters and numerals) to the central processing unit (CPU), a mainframe, or very large computer shared by many users. (In those days, mainframes tended to be room-sized.)

As early as the late 1940s, punched Hollerith (so-called IBM) cards were used in large academic libraries for book circulation records. Other early routine functions handled by computers were essentially comparison or counting tasks, such as ordering, analyzing circulation, and various serials operations. Meanwhile, library business offices discovered the computer's facility for compiling statistical data and reports, and for what became known as word processing.

While circulation was the earliest function to be automated, it was quickly followed by the automated creation of catalog records and the compilation of catalogs. Initially, the output of the batch mode was printed out on formidable stacks of green-lined paper or converted into microfiche (or COM, Computer Output Micrograph) catalogs. These were card-sized films requiring a specialized reader.

The shift to directly readable bibliographic records began in 1965 at the Library of Congress with the development of the MARC (Machine Readable Cataloging) program. Since 1971, LC-MARC (later, USMARC) has been subject to the American (ANSI and NISO) standard Z39.2, the international version of which is ISO 2709.[4] Also in the 60s, OCLC, Inc., the first of the online bibliographic utilities, began operations.[5] The OCLC created, in effect, an online (rather than print-based) union catalog as a source of cataloging copy, of catalog cards, and of bibliographic and interlibrary loan data.

Another important library use of computer technology is the online searching of other databases. Online searches—sometimes faster, certainly more flexible than using the paper indexes upon which the datasets are based—widen the library's bibliographic net far beyond the library site. The first of these bibliographic databases was developed in the 1960s by Lockheed to facilitate the journal searches made by its engineers.

Database use is now widespread; for many libraries, despite costs in fees and connect (telephone long distance) time, it is time-saving and cost-effective. The increased power of search engines means that the World Wide Web is becoming a source of once-print-only resources, such as Grove's *Dictionary of Art,* available (by subscription) at: http://www.grovereference.com.

With the introduction of step-by-step database software programs for personal computers, librarians have created locally searchable databases tailored to local needs, thus giving patrons access, for example, to a librarian-created index to regional newspapers.

Thus library computerization has progressed in less than a half century from batch-mode punched cards to the interactive system linking user and database through a terminal, keyboard and telecommunications. More particularly, the introduction of the affordable PC has made automation a true possibility even for small libraries. Introduction of the software to link PCs into local area networks (LANs) has superannuated the mainframe in many organizations. Now one CPU becomes the server, or data source, and the organization's other PCs are linked to it.

A parallel growth in the use of computers has occurred in museums. In the beginning, large computers and their benefits were limited to large institutions with the resources and means to invest in the new methodologies. Programs for registration systems were written for mainframe computers: SELGEM, GRIPHOS, NEPHIS, and others. Some programs, such as the Detroit Art Institute's DARIS, included library materials. More often, however, the individual organization created a unique computerized system, reinventing the registration wheel time after time for mainframe after mainframe or—as they became as powerful as the early mainframes—desktop after desktop. And each new system tended to emphasize the generation of reports rather than the uniformity of record structure.[6]

More recently in museums, as has been the case in libraries, the PC and the online environment have led to external links and some increase in data uniformity as museums struggle with the dichotomies between unique collections and their unique attributes and the universal information needs of the wider museum community.

Computer Systems

Nearly every library operation has been touched by automation. In general, there are three approaches to automation: the integrated system; the distributed system, and the internal network—LAN and intranet.

The integrated system depends upon an interrelated set of programs and a central inventory database—and usually the memory and storage capacity of a mainframe computer—for the data processing. Thus acquisitions, serials, cataloging, circulation, and inventory use related software and the same bibliographic database housed on a mainframe.

In the mainframe world, computer-sharing is common. Libraries under public governance often share a computer with other government agencies and departments, and academic libraries sometimes share computers with college or university administrative offices. At the same time, the PC, with its variety of software, has become such an affordable and versatile tool that agencies with fully integrated systems supplement the mainframe with personal computers for many tasks.

The distributed system can use a large computer to store the bibliographic records for an online catalog and other hardware—usually PCs—to perform such tasks as serials control, acquisitions and ordering, or circulation. The distributed system can also use a local area network (LAN) with a central file server (in effect, a subset database). Such a system does not link all library functions together.

This type of system has disadvantages; for example, some data are stored twice and not all data are retrievable from the same terminal. On the other hand, when one component breaks down, not all library functions are affected. When vendor-supplied software or hardware is used, some operations, such as ordering books, subscribing to serials, and contracting for binding stand alone in the configuration, although the resulting records are later incorporated into the database.

The trend now is increasingly to decentralized systems; the library is no longer tied to a mainframe.[7] While dispensing with the mainframe, the intranet links the computers in one site together as a network, with one designated to be the server that hosts the databases and programs accessed by the other computers in the network.

Museums and larger libraries are finding this arrangement to be a workable solution, relieving them of being at the mercy of central hardware and its software requirements. Additionally, the individual desktops are less expensive, because their memory capacity need not be as large. This same trend has encouraged outsourcing, the sending out of standardized tasks such as cataloging, and serials acquisitions and control.[8]

In museums, powerful PCs and LAN systems have also increased the popularity of the museum management software packages, which are designed to serve the needs of collections management, membership, accounting, and so on. Several include library modules, but—and here a word of warning—*the library modules are not all MARC-compatible.* Adapting idiosyncratic records to an ISBD/MARC-based catalog may take more tweaking than the librarian has time for.

Uses for Automation

Data and information retrieval. The online retrieval of data and information involves a commitment of fees and telecommunication service, including installation of a modem (modulator-demodulator), which translates telephone signals to computer input and vice versa. The costs of online service must be measured, of course, against the costs of purchasing and maintaining a number of paper indexes and reference resources, of librarian and museum staff time devoted to manual searches, and of failure to have needed data.

Since a dedicated, single-use terminal is no longer required as once it was, any modem-equipped desktop computer in the museum can be used for searching online databases, raising the potential for conflicting purposes when online activity reduces the availability of the machine. The obvious solution is for the museum library to have its own terminal and modem.

There are ways of keeping search costs down. The most important strategy is to prepare carefully, formulating the search as fully as possible before connecting with the database. If a large volume of searching is anticipated, or if the cooperative online service proves unexpectedly popular once inaugurated, another option may lie in off-hour special rates offered by some services. Such rates, together with educational discounts, which can sometimes be negotiated, bring down the costs of online data searching.

When the librarian is ready to subscribe to an online service, the vendor's proposal and contract should be carefully scrutinized, not so much because vendors are dishonest, but because they have a natural entrepreneurial desire to sell as much service as possible. Such desires have led to initially low-cost subscriptions that bump up at renewal time, bundling of databases when a museum library may require only one or two, and per-search add-on charges.[9]

If it is initially not economically feasible for the library to have its own computer, and the research needs of the museum staff require online services, there are alternative solutions, as noted in chapter 6. One is a cooperative arrangement with another special library. In some arrangements, the requesting library simply pays the search costs; in others, a consortium will share the pro-rated costs of the service, including database fees and online time. Another solution is to contract for the services of an information broker or an online search service. Still another alternative is to subscribe to the appropriate database in CD-ROM format—after, of course, a careful cost comparison with the same or similar database in online format. Some degree of currency is lost in the CD-ROM alternative, since the updates usually come monthly or even quarterly. As Quint reminds us, the purchase price of CD-ROMs is not considered licensing, so the vendor should not require previous issues be returned.[10]

Catalog card copy and production. The second frequent library use of online databases is to secure cataloging copy or MARC records,[11] from which catalog cards can be made, or to locate sources of catalog cards. (See Appendix D for a fuller discussion of copy cataloging sources.) The online bibliographic utilities, such as OCLC, are sources of both cataloging copy and catalog cards.

Unless a cooperative or consortium arrangement can be made with other special libraries in the area, the small museum library is unlikely to have sufficient volume to warrant the expense of network membership for card production. However, the library can purchase the less-expensive search-only capability to locate cataloging copy. More recently, the Internet has become a major source of cataloging copy; many library catalogs are found there, including that of the Library of Congress (LOC) (http://lcweb.loc.gov/catalog).

Membership in a bibliographic network, with its access to MARC records, should be kept in long-range planning, because changes and developments in the MARC format for audio-visual materials have accommodated three-dimensional objects as well as other media.[12] Now the integrated, all-media MARC format means it will be possible for museums to use a bibliographic utility, such as OCLC, both for bibliographic control functions in the library and for the registration and cataloging of their object collections.[13] Network membership would then become cost-effective.

Once the cataloging copy is secured, the librarian or library assistant can create the cards for the catalog, typing the primary access from the bibliographic data, and then the other cards (title, subject, and so forth) for the set. There are also card-production software packages for the PC. These programs automatically produce sets of cards from menu-driven screen instructions. They are probably the best version of cataloging automation available for the paper-based museum library. The programs can be used by library assistants and volunteers who have been trained to recognize the components of a title page and to place those elements in the proper fields of title statement, publisher, and so on. The best of the cataloging software packages produce records that conform to MARC standards. Some versions have a down-loading capability, which helps prepare for an online catalog. A word of caution, however: the printer serving the PC must be sufficiently heavy-duty to accommodate card stock. (Again, see Appendix D.)

OPAC (Online Public Access Catalog). Proceeding from card to online cat-alog requires a drastic change in cataloging procedures, from typing sets of cards to creating (or downloading) MARC records. Sometimes the library "freezes" the card catalog, leaving it just as it was on a particular day and then picking up on the following day with subsequent acquisitions appearing in the OPAC sys-tem. This decision means, of course, that library staff and patrons have two cat-alogs to search.

Another strategy, known as *retrospective conversion*, goes back in time to convert the paper records to MARC format for the electronic environment. Given sufficient staff or volunteer time and training, "recon" can be accomplished in-house. Library support service companies such as Brodart sell CD-ROM data-bases especially for in-house conversion. Another solution is to outsource the project, contracting it out to a conversion service.[14] (The Library of Congress lists MARC retrospective conversion services at http://lcweb.loc.gov/cds/selmarl.html [accessed August 2000].) The resulting MARC records are stored on the PC hard drive (in the case of a small collection), or on a server or mainframe. It is also possible to have the library's records converted to CD-ROM. Updates must be part of the contract, but new records can only be added on a new disc; thus records cannot be added as frequently and readily as in the hard or floppy disk computer systems. The limitations of read-only memory (ROM) will be over-come when recordable CDs are widely available.

There are also various online catalog software package systems on the mar-ket, many of which require considerable drive capacity. Ideally, the library should select the catalog software on the basis of its suitability to the collection, rather than its compatibility with whatever museum hardware the library may share. Of course, if the library already has an adequate computer, such considerations become moot.

To search the OPAC, the library patron uses the same search keys—author name, title, or subject—as he or she used when thumbing through the card catalog, and the search results displayed on the screen can be programmed to mimic closely the familiar ISBD card record. For a while there was some dis-cussion about card-like *vs.* tagged displays (in which the various fields in the record are labeled according to their content).[15] However, more and more libraries are using labeled displays, of which the Library of Congress online records are a good example. Standards for OPAC display are being developed and promul-gated.

Database and information management software. The desktop owner is the beneficiary of a cornucopia of software products of various design, intent, and levels of success. Because of the plethora of local materials in a history library, the critical and specialized data needed in a science library, or the array of media and objects found in an industrial arts collection, the management of such data is critical to the success of the library; thus the software for in-house databases is often more critical than that for the more standardized online catalog.

The simplest program allows one to create a list and then locate data in the list by using a *search key*, or matching element, such as a name, word, title, or code. The more complex relational databases permit the joining and association of data under interrelated headings and the location of data through linking search keys in different patterns. Hypermedia systems enable the searcher to move about the database with great speed and facility. Initially confined to the Apple MacIntosh, hypermedia software is now available for other kinds of computers, but is giving way to the links and buttons of HTML, or hypertext mark-up language. Once again, the mission of the museum and the means by which the library plans to support that mission will determine the extent and type of datafiles the library will develop and maintain.

Vocabulary control and error detection are datafile imperatives. Without them, datafiles become one with the ether. For example, if the library's catalog uses PETS as a subject heading, the index to the vertical file should not substitute HOUSEHOLD ANIMALS without, at least, a cross-reference. And if keyword searching is used, check keywords and authors' name for spelling errors. Imported records, even those from the Library of Congress, have such errors as *Ogdon* as the spelling for *Ogden*. As Ballard notes, the Web is in even worse shape, orthographically.[17]

The Internet in the library. No discussion of technology in the library is complete without a bow to the Internet, the hypermedium of hypermedia. From relatively modest beginnings as a communication system among scientists, and then among academics, it exploded in the late 1990s to a vast lacework of sites and links in which the most staid and sober-sided of corporations wrapped themselves because of their very real fear of being left out of the coming age of e-commerce.[17]

The non-commercial visitor to the Internet finds electronic services, chats, and bulletin boards that bring together persons with similar interests who are geographically dispersed. It also provides access to the online catalogs of many large libraries and even to some museum libraries. In fact, many museums now have a Web site presence on the Internet.

While the commercial uses of the Internet may seem removed from museum libraries (except, perhaps, for ordering books or supplies), they will have a long-term effect. For one thing, information once offered for free (or for the price of viewing some advertising) is now subject to restrictions such as registration (for example, the new online version of the *New York Times*), and outright subscription. As Web sites proliferate, the choice of search engines, browsers, and indexing will be increasingly important to the task of locating data or information.[18] And so will the standby skills of research and validation, inasmuch as the Internet is a huge information democracy, with good and bad information equally accessible. It is also an international phenomenon—an information democracy without national borders.

Meanwhile, librarians have viewed the Internet with professional and not entirely disinterested alarm. As long ago as 1994, scientists were warning that

> Internet information is growing faster than the ability to keep up with it.... [It] resembles an enormous used book store with volumes stacked on shelves and tables and overflowing on the floor, and a continuous stream of new books being added helter-skelter to the piles.[19]

The National Science Foundation was then proposing "electronic helpers" to locate Internet contents, rather than a central catalog. The helpers, which became browsers, have proven not entirely adequate to the task of accurately and quickly locating sites and their content; retrieval rates are estimated at one-third.[20] Whether, as Martin Dillon suggests, it is too late to catalog the Internet,[21] there are current attempts to get a handle on it and its contents. One is the so-called Dublin Core (Dublin Metadata Core Element Set), "a first attempt at developing a common group of elements that could be used consistently to describe networked information resources."[22] In structure, it lies between full-text Web indexes and MARC.[23]

Conceptually, the Internet—like other complex sources that point to resources and to pointers that point to pointers of resources—is a set of metadata, or data about data—encoded locators, as it were. Anyone who has searched for the home page of a particular museum and, after an inordinate wait, been triumphantly offered a choice of 3,246 museums (because the search system homed in on the term *museum*), can only wish well those engaged in developing the Dublin Core, or any other such effort. There are also some "big catalog" projects being undertaken to archive those super-ephemeral, the Web sites.[24]

The Internet environment is literally changing daily. Amid and alongside the original flow of the scholarly and objective, we see the ill-informed and ignorant, while Internet companies merge like amoeba, dine on one another like jungle denizens, and otherwise tend to their primeval struggle to survive and even prosper.

The Internet spectacle is fascinating to watch, but the librarian must be a wary watcher, alert to the changes, ready to take advantage of the riches, and cautious about becoming enmeshed.[25] As a revolution in communication, the Internet has been compared to many things, including the printing press. And like the earlier librarians who were amazed at printed books without realizing where the relative trickle would take them, we can only speculate at the outcome of the electronic messages daily crackling on our desktops.

In Summary

With PCs installed in museum offices and laboratories, computerization is an increasingly viable technology for the museum library. Certainly, library and information services which support the museum's mission and functions can make a case for equal participation in the automation of routines and production procedures.

In the final analysis, however, the technological *how* is less important than the bibliographical and informational *what*—the library and information services accessible to the museum community. Technologies, then, must be evaluated on the basis of whether and how they will advance the mission of the museum and museum library. A few caveats to post on the PC (or its future site):

1. *Technology is a tool; it will bestow no magic and will not cure what ails.* It can be as complex and versatile as a Swiss army knife or as simple and direct as a crochet hook. Technology does not, to be useful, have to be electronic; indeed, certain electronic capabilities may be more than the library can comfortably handle at the beginning. Other kinds of technology should be used, however, if they will free the librarian and library assistants to perform information services, which support the museum and its staff.

2. *Vigilance is the price of technological knowledge; tomorrow's developments will not be like today's, and certainly not like yesterday's.* The librarian needs to keep current with and aware of the broad developments in automation and computerization by reading software reviews, asking about the experiences of other special librarians, and sending for demonstration disks and documentation about software. The librarian should also keep both the administration and the board informed of developments and changes that will affect planning.

3. *Today's planning guards against being blindsided by tomorrow's surprises.* The librarian needs to be aware of the short- and long-term probabilities for computerization. Such awareness means that the staff has considered various systems configurations, hardware, and software, and the sequence, if necessary, in which automation might be introduced. Options for automation, whether achieved in stages or all at once, and intermediate solutions such as cooperative online retrieval should also be planned carefully. Awareness also means that paper systems are carefully designed for ready conversion to electronic format: by the use of ISBD-based, MARC-compatible bibliographic records, for example; and by careful authority control that eliminates duplicate index terms.

Save for the small, rather static, and highly specialized museum library, computerization is inevitable, and it should be welcomed with open arms—but also with open eyes. Even as they make their plans for the collection, catalog, and services, the staff in the paper-based library that is starting-up or revitalizing will need to plan also for a wired-up and interconnected future.

Only those who haven't been there could possibly think that librarianship is dull and boring!

Notes

1. James R. Blackaby, "On Learning to Use a New Appliance," *Museum News* 66/6 (July/August 1988): 33.

2. Richard Buchen, "A Survey of Museums and Historical Societies to Determine Interest in Computer Networking," *Spectra: The International Journal of Computer Applications in Museums* 16/4 (Winter 1989): 5–7.

3. Brian Nielsen, "Technological Change and Professional Identity," in *New Information Technologies—New Opportunities* (Urbana-Champaign: University of Illinois Graduate School of Library and Information Science, 1982), pp. 101–113. Eighteen years later, this attitude lingers as demonstrated in the reverence for Internet findings, discussed in Tina Kelley, "Whales in the Minnesota River?" *New York Times* (Thursday, 4 March 1999): D4.

4. Actually a family of communication formats, MARC also contains formats for transmitting data for name authority, subject authority, and classification, among others.

5. The OCLC began its pre-computerized existence as the Ohio College Library Consortium. After several name permutations required by rapid growth outside Ohio, the acronym now stands for Online Computer Library Center, Inc.

6. Richard B. Light *et al.*, *Museum Documentation Systems* (London: Butterworth's, 1986), p. 10.

7. Robert Klepper, and Wendell O. Jones, *Outsourcing Information Technology, Systems, and Services* (Upper Saddle River, N.J.: Prentice Hall, 1998), p. 26.

8. Klepper, *Outsourcing*, p. 27.

9. Barbara Quint, "More Practices We'd Like to See Less," *Information Today* 16/6 (June, 1999): 12–13; 69.

10. Quint, "More Practices," p. 69.

11. The simplest, yet complete, explanation of the MARC bibliographic format is to be found in a small booklet distributed by the Library of Congress: Betty Furrie, *Understanding MARC Bibliographic: Machine-Readable Cataloging*, 5th ed. (Washington, D. C.: Library of Congress, Network Development and MARC Standards Office, 1998; originally copyrighted by the Follett Software Company, 1988, 1989, 1990).

12. Esther Green Bierbaum, "MARC in Museums: Applicability of the Revised Visual Materials Format," *Information Technology and Libraries* 9/4 (December 1990): 291–299.

13. Appearing in the Fall of 1999, MARC 21 incorporated the cumulative changes to the MARC format, as well as the harmonization of USMARC and the Canadian variant, CAN/MARC.

14. Technical services are often good candidates for outsourcing. Costs and downtime balanced against outside expertise and better use of library staff talents are among the considerations. See Karen A. Wilson, and Marylou Colver, eds., *Outsourcing Library Technical Services Operations: Practices in Academic, Public and Special Libraries* (Chicago: ALA, 1997).

15. Walt Crawford, "Testing Bibliographic Displays for Online Catalogs," *Information Technology and Libraries* 6/3 (September 1987): 20–33.

16. Terry Ballard, "Systems Librarian: The Rest of the Story," *Information Today* 16/3 (March 1999): 52–53.

17. For a nontechnical account of the beginnings of the Internet and how to use it, see Ed Krol, *The Whole Internet: User's Guide & Catalog*, 1st and 2nd editions (Sebastopol, Calif.: O'Reilly & Associates, 1992 and 1994.) Recent developments in the commercialization of the Internet are not, of course, addressed at all.

18. Donald J. Sager, "John Henry versus the Computer: The Impact of the Internet on Reference Service," *Public Libraries* 38/1 (January/February 1999): 21–25.

19. Robert Pool, "Turning an Info-Glut Into a Library," *Science* 266 (7 October 1994): 20–22.

20. "Marginalia," *The Chronicle of Higher Education* 44 (22 May 1998): A8.

21. Norman Oder, "Cataloging the Net: Can We Do It?" *Library Journal* 123/16 (1 October 1998): 47–51.

22. Jim Blackaby, and Beth Sandore. "Building Integrated Museum Information and Retrieval Systems," *Archives and Museum Informatics* 11/2 (1997): 117–146; and see also the Website for the Dublin Core, http://purl.oclc.org/metadata/dublin_core (accessed August 2000).

23. Blackaby and Sandore, "Building Integrated," p. 126.

24. Carol Casey, "The Cyberarchive: A Look at the Storage and Preservation of Web Sites," *College & Research Libraries* 59/4 (July 1998): 304–307.

25. For some practical advice on keeping up with the Internet, see Susan Fingerman, "Faster Than a Speeding Bullet (or, How to Keep Up with the Internet," *Information Outlook* 3/5 (May 1999): 19–22. For other information, see the Krol titles listed in "Further Reading" for this chapter.

Further Reading

Technology and Automation

Barnett, Patricia J., and Amy E. Lucker, eds. *Procedural Guide to Automating an Art Library*. Tucson, Ariz.: ARLIS/NA, 1987. (Occasional Papers of the Art Libraries Society of North America, no. 7.)

Bearman, David, and John Perkins. *Standards Framework for the Computer Interchange of Museum Information*. Silver Spring, Md.: Museum Computer Network (MCN), Computer Interchange of Museum Information Committee (CIMI), 1993.

Bills, Linda G. "Making Decisions About Automation for Small Libraries." *Library Resources and Technical Services* 29/2 (April/June 1985): 161–171.

Blackaby, Jim, and Beth Sandore. "Building Integrated Museum Information Retrieval Systems: Practical Approaches to Data Organization." *Archives and Museum Informatics* 11/2 (1997): 117–146.

Caswell, Lucy Shelton. "Item Level Access to Special Collections: A Prototype for an Integrated Automated Index." *Journal of Library Administration* 15/3-4 (1991): 101–120.

Clark, David L. *Database Design: Applications of Library Cataloging Techniques.* [New York]: McGraw-Hill, 1991.

Curator 30/2 (June 1987): Whole issue on computers in museums.

Light, Robert B., *et al.*, eds. *Museum Documentation Systems: Development and Applications.* London: Boston: Butterworths, 1986.

Orna, Elizabeth, and Charles Pettitt. Foreword by Max Hebditch. *Information Management in Museums.* 2nd ed. Aldershot, Hants (England); Broomfield, Vermont: Gower, 1998.

Porter, M.F. *A Unified Approach to the Computerization of Museum Catalogues.* London: British Library, 1977. (British Library Research and Development Reports, no. 5338.)

Summers, John E. "The Computerized Cataloguing of Historic Watercraft: A Case Study in Information Retrieval in Museology." *Journal of the American Society for Information Science* 40/4 (July 1989): 253–261.

Williams, David W. *A Guide to Museum Computing.* Nashville, Tenn.: AASLH, 1987.

The many museum and library/information science journals are valuable resources for keeping up with current trends in automation. Among them are *Art Documentation, Computers in Libraries, Information Today, Information Outlook, Information Technology and Libraries, Journal of the American Society for Information Science (JASIS), Library Hi-Tech, Library Resources & Technical Services, Spectra, Technical Services Quarterly,* and *Technicalities.* There are also computer magazines such as: *Family Computing, InfoWorld, PC Magazine, PC Tech Journal,* and *PC World.*

MARC and Other Formats

Byrne, Deborah J. *MARC Manual: Understanding and Using MARC Records.* Englewood, Col.: Libraries Unlimited, 1991.

Consortium for the Computer Interchange of Museum Information (CIMI). Available at http://www.cimi.org. (Also see Bearman, David, above.)

Cox, Richard. "The American Archival Profession and Information Technology Standards." *Journal of the American Society for Information Science* 43/8 (September 1992): 571–575.

"Dublin Core Metadata": http://purl.oclc.org/metadata/dublin_core (accessed August 2000).

Furrie, Betty. *Understanding MARC Bibliographic: Machine-Readable Cataloging.* 5th ed. Washington, D. C.: Library of Congress, Network Development and MARC Standards Office, 1998; originally copyrighted by the Follett Software Company, 1988, 1989, 1990.

Hensen, Steven L. *Archives, Personal Papers, and Manuscripts (APPM): A Cataloging Manual for Archival Repositories, Historical Societies, and Manuscript Libraries.* 2nd ed. Chicago: SAA, 1989.

Library of Congress, Network Development, and MARC Standards Office. *MARC 21 Format for Bibliographic Data: Including Guidelines for Content Designation.* Washington, D.C.: Library of Congress, in cooperation with Standards and Support, National Library of Canada, 1999. [Supersedes the 1994 ed. and 1995–1997 updates.]

Library of Congress, Network Development, and MARC Standards Office. *MARC21 Concise Formats*. Washington, D.C.: Library of Congress, 2000. [Brings all MARC formats together.]

Library of Congress, Network Development, and MARC Standards Office. *Format Integration and its Effect on the USMARC Bibliographic Format*. Washington, D.C.: Library of Congress, 1995.

Museum Documentation Association (MDA). *Data Definition Language and Data Standards*. Duxford, Cambridgeshire (England): MDA, 1980; 1985.

Tatem, Jill. "Beyond USMARC AMC: The Context of Data Exchange Format." *Midwestern Archivist* 14/1(1989): 39–48.

The Internet

Krol, Ed. *The Whole Internet User's Guide & Catalog*. Academic ed., adapted by Bruce C. Klopfenstein. Belmont, Calif.: Integra Media Group; Sebastopol, Calif.: O'Reilly, 1996.

_____. *The Whole Internet User's Guide & Catalog*. 2nd ed. Sebastopol, Calif.: O'Reilly, 1994.

Ladner, Sharyn J., and Hope N. Tillman. *The Internet and Special Libraries: Use, Training and the Future*. SLA Research Series, #10. Washington, D.C.: SLA, 1993.

Pool, Robert. "Turning an Info-Glut into a Library." *Science* 266 (7 October 1994): 20–22.

Sager, Donald J. "John Henry versus the Computer: The Impact of the Internet on Reference Service." *Public Libraries* 38/1 (January/February 1999): 21–25.

Chapter 9

Partnership:
Libraries and Museums

The basic assumption of this book has been that the library *in* the museum is—or should be—an integral element in the message the museum offers to visitors. This message grows out of the subject area and collections of the museum. When well conveyed and received, the message becomes information about the seashore, or certain artists, or electricity, or a particular community.

The museum library enriches this information process for the visitor, most often indirectly by providing information to the museum staff; sometimes directly by providing it in person to the visitor. But what is the nature of this information that we all speak of so glibly?

Mutual Matters:
Data and Information

Data and information are coin of the realm for both museums and libraries. Whether as participants or as observers, we tend to discuss information as though it were a commodity, like potatoes, or a good, like happiness. Rather often, we talk about "information" when we actually mean "data," understanding the connotation anyway. But in the realm of museums, and of libraries and information services, it is useful to make a distinction between *data* and *information*, a distinction based on the size of the unit in question, the use to which the unit is put, and the inquirer's perceptions of it.

Data are the smallest pieces of communication; they are discrete units or facts. They come in various forms: names, dates, sets of numerals that may represent, perhaps, girth, or weight, or distance.

Data usually require interpretation; that is, they do not convey information except when placed within a context or accompanied by some explanation.[1] For example, the numerals 2 and 4 can represent the date of a month, someone's age, the distance to Columbus, Ohio, or the air temperature in centigrade degrees. Even relating the numerals to a concept (such as date or distance) is not always enough to provide a context. To make much sense of the numerical date, we need to know the name of the month, the identity of the person, the starting point of the journey, or the time of day and season of the year.

Data often are presented in data sets: (45, 58), (32, 45). Again, until placed in a context these sets remain numerals without ascertainable meaning. But if our museum reports that this year 45 people participated in the bird count and 58 attended the Arbor Day planting, whereas last year, 32 participated in the bird count and 45 attended Arbor Day, then we have given the data sets significance: they convey the information that this year saw greater attendance than last—perhaps because this year's weather was finer or the publicity was better. (Good data lead to researchable questions.)

Information, then, consists of data within a context, data enhanced with what is (to us) significance. The reader has probably experienced the distinction between data and information in the course of gathering article titles from a periodical index. One's hand-written list or the printout from a bibliographic database contained numerous potentially useful titles; but one still has to seek out the articles themselves to glean information about the subject of interest. The list or printout of articles were data sets; the information was the result of reading and thinking about the articles.[2] This is why database searching, or "information retrieval," is often more accurately a matter of data retrieval.[3]

Individuals who make significant use of data create information for themselves or others. But information is not equal. The quality of information depends on several factors. Foremost is the accuracy of the data. We have all experienced the consequences of basing actions on faulty data, such as the time shown by a slow clock. Economic, military, and social decisions are daily made on the basis of poor data. For example, Hitler's incomplete assessment of the Russian defenses resulted in disaster for his troops. Equally disastrous results can come from ignoring or not believing good data, as in the case of the events leading to the Three Mile Island nuclear accident and the *Challenger* disaster.[4]

Many museums are having to re-evaluate information that was based on faulty data. Even in the world of science, as Thomas S. Kuhn demonstrated, data are constantly reassessed until a new model results.[5]

Another factor in information quality is the background of the data receivers: the other data sets they have previously encountered; the information they have already derived; the baggage of experience, need, and personal quirks they bring to the encounter. We cannot assume, for instance, that every visitor's sense of history is the same, or even that he works from the same knowledge base. While data and information providers often have little control over what their patrons carry along with them, the providers—museums, schools, libraries, radio stations—can and do try to find out more about their patrons and prepare the context of the data accordingly. Thus a museum staff, aware of what visitors can or cannot be expected to know, will develop a context and setting for an exhibited object—perhaps a timeline linking Revolutionary-era household goods to the same time period in other countries.

The quality of information has many consequences. If it is useful and meaningful, it can help solve a problem, furnish some momentary but memorable pleasure, or be carefully stored for the future. The information derived from an exhibit demonstrating pond siltation from run-off may be retrieved later when the visitor votes in a zoning referendum. Such information enriches our lives; and after we put enough together, our *knowledge* in some field may be increased. Enough knowledge, carefully nurtured and viewed through the prism of experience, may even bring us *wisdom*. However, the development of information and the increase of knowledge are more realistic goals for a museum than fostering wisdom.

Cartoon by Sidney Harris.

Information of the opposite sort—incomplete, false, or wrong because of bad data or the disinformation and misinformation resulting from falsely manipulated data—also has consequences. Having bad information is potentially worse than lacking information. The situation is worse again when the information-seeker depends on another party or agency for context and significance. Trust, the development of knowledge, intellectual freedom, and the worth of the individual are diminished in the encounter with false and misleading information. Voters, for example, may feel used and abused when they discover false statements have been made by an official.

As we have noted, museums have become increasingly aware of their responsibilities in presenting, evaluating, and interpreting data. Reattribution, careful statements of provenance, and exhibits that present a variety of data and viewpoints are all ways of dealing with the ethical issues of possibly contaminated data and information.

An underlying thesis of this book is that the museum's value to the community is greater than the sum of its parts, that the organization as a whole should transmit the museum's message about its collections—that is, it should act as a system.

Museums as Information Systems

A *system* is a set of functions or functional units that, working together in a predetermined pattern, produces an outcome, whether product or service. A restaurant, from the hostess through the servers, cooks, chef, and cashier, is an interactive meal production system, not simply a dining area and kitchen. And, likewise, the museum is an *information system* rather than a conglomeration of spaces—workrooms, storage areas, exhibits, classrooms and offices—or a gathering of functions and departments—membership, or bookkeeping, or education, or exhibits, with communication going on within and between the parts.[6]

Systems may be linear: step A; then step B; leading to outcome C. More often, however, they resemble a network, with various internal communications taking place as needed. In the restaurant, for example, the interplay of communication involves diners, servers, chef, and cooks in a predictable pattern, but one which allows data exchanges such as <<French fries = 0>>, and results in diner satisfaction and a repeat customer. In agencies such as a museum, the coinage of reward is less tangible and measurable, but real nonetheless: visitors who take new information, or even knowledge, with them.

When we speak of information in the museum, we are dealing with something quite specific: accurate and reliable data that can be given context and meaning, and transformed into information. The information, in turn, can fill an intellectual, recreational, or emotional need.

In the successful museum, the transformation is not a happenstance. The context is created when a staff member or volunteer arranges data—objects, images, cards, papers—in a meaningful and significant way, whether in an exhibit, a file, a cabinet, or a notebook. The completion of the transformation comes when the information is received or retrieved—when the visitor thinks about the message of the exhibit, when the curator finds evidence to support his research thesis.

When the transformation leads to the visitor's "Aha!" of enlightenment and delight or to the curator's "Gotcha!" of discovery, the receiver is then in the position to pass along the information to others. And the museum library and its information services are integral links in this communication and information system we call the museum.

The support of mission is an integrative principle. When the departments and functions of the museum focus, for example, upon "the collection, study and preservation of the objects associated with the history of the Middle Valley region, and the interpretation of that history to the region's citizens through the meaningful exhibition of selected objects," the museum becomes an information system about Middle Valley, the parts working together to become greater than their sum.

The concept of coherence within a system is important for the museum's well-being and future. Questions raised by various issues such as security, blockbuster exhibits, and the sale of objects to support operations have at times meant a loss of public credibility.[7] There is some question whether museums are still the engines of culture, part of the alabaster cities, of the last century[8]—however thinly the cultural jam may have been spread on the public bread. When John C. Dana urged that museums go and take lessons from the great department stores (which certainly were imbued with a mission), he recognized that a sugared glaze was not enough; people also needed solid stuff, a meaningful context in which to be enlightened and to learn.[9]

Yet museums still wrestle with an ancient and basic dichotomy: obligations to the objects and obligations to the public. Without a coherent vision of the museum's mission, the first obligation may preclude the second, and those who care for and study the objects may seem to be in conflict with the programs of those who interpret the objects to the public in exhibits and instruction.[10] Thus when there are different versions of mission under the same roof, the museum is a house divided. But when the museum is an information system, the coherence of mission is more easily maintained so that the observance of the obligation of caring for the objects leads to discharging the second obligation, that of interpretation, which leads in turn to satisfying the public's curiosity about local history; and the public's information needs—educational, aesthetic, or recreational—are served.

Partnership

For the community to realize and benefit from the full potential of museums and libraries working together, there are three principal issues and concerns which need to be addressed:

- the role of library and information services in the museum information system;
- the exchange of data within the museum
- the accessibility of museum data and information from outside the museum.

Libraries in Museums

The role and place of the library in the museum must be recognized at all levels. It is, however, a role that is earned. This book has attempted to explain why and how to accomplish that end. As an entity within the system, the museum library first, and most basically, is not at liberty to go swooping off in its own orbit, and then later bemoan a lack of institutional support.

The obverse of the coin is that, while library support of the museum's mission comes first for the library, there must be a mission to support. As we have noted, the communication of a coherent vision is the responsibility of the board and museum administration.

For the most part, visitors are unaware of the library's role behind the scenes, even though the data or information provided by the library have assisted museum staff members in their study, preservation, and interpretation of objects, and have thus helped the visitors to increase their store of information and enhance their understanding of, in our example, Middle Valley. Yet it is a small and not unreasonable gesture, for instance, to acknowledge the library's contribution to an exhibit or program. Authors of books do so; why not curators and exhibit designers? Of such gestures are communities built, and for the librarian, such recognition relates the library and information services to the rest of the activities and functions which work together in the museum.

Reinforcing the centrality of library services is also a prime argument for visitor access to the library. As John C. Dana—an old library hand himself—observed,

> It would be difficult to find a point in time, in the life of any visitor who has shown a lively interest...when a book would be as useful to him as when he has just been examining the collections which attract him.[11]

The library should, indeed, earn its place on both the museum's signs and Web site, but such recognition should be readily given by museum administrators.

Data Exchange

A second issue, one more technical but no less philosophical or important, is the exchange of data within the museum. In practical terms, data exchange means that curators or exhibit designers should be able to search an in-house database from a terminal in their departments to determine the library's holdings on a particular subject or in a specific run of journals. Similarly, the librarian should be able to locate at the library's terminal the objects—type specimens of mosses, say, or arrowheads—which would augment the information a patron has gleaned from reading.

However, in the paper-based museum, the library harbors one set of file drawers, and the collections activities, one or more other sets; data exchange is largely a matter of going and finding the right drawer. To merge the files—much less duplicate them—is unthinkable, philosophically as well as physically and economically.

But paper-based attitudes need not be carried into the electronic environment; nor should they eternally control even paper files. There have been two difficulties with museum computerization, one personal, the other, mechanical. Of the first, Blackaby notes,

> Holders of museum information, whether curators or registrars or even exhibition specialists or educators, are often reluctant to relinquish control over their data.[12]

Here is another instance of Davenport's "information politics."

The second difficulty has been that software has been hardware-specific or site specialized, not to mention oriented toward production of reports rather than creation of records. Yet, as Elizabeth Orna points out,

> the importance of the record cannot be over-estimated; it represents the object and so carries a central responsibility in any system of handling information.[13]

A beginning step, then, toward data exchange within the museum is the in-house standardization of object and bibliographic records so that each set, lodged in its database on a mainframe or server, can be accessed from terminals throughout the museum and library. While a less-elegant solution than a seamless melding of both datasets, this sort of project gets the job done, often with the hardware available.

In past years I have advocated the MARC communications format as the records structure for both bibliographic and objects collections; and, with the advent of MARC 21, it is still a feasible solution for smaller collections. The next few years will decide whether the Dublin Core, developing along with MARC, will be the metadata key to unlocking the puzzle of varying record structures used to describe electronic resources.[14]

But life is not simple, as the authors in *The Wired Museum* take rueful pains to point out.[15] Technology and data conversion on an institution-wide basis require careful planning and whole-hearted cooperation.[16] But whatever the records solution within the organization, the librarian and the library, as essential traders in the data and information coinage, should—indeed, must—be included.

Beyond the Walls

The third issue goes beyond the museum's walls to universal access to descriptive data about museum collections. Libraries have historically shared collection data and collections; international bibliographic databases such as OCLC have shown the possibilities for universally accessible library union catalogs. Reasonably, we should have the same access capabilities for museum catalogs as we have for library catalogs. Bibliographic and object catalogs could even be linked in national databases, in the same way OCLC has included some museum collections in its database.

However, letting the world know what is in the collection has not historically been a *sine qua non* for museums; indeed, if anything, a certain competitive spirit has kept that data under wraps. But times have changed, and the towering change agent has been the Internet. Museums are now telling their stories and showing examples from their collections on Web pages, and selling CD-ROMs of the "museum experience" on the Web as well as in the gift shop. Meanwhile some museum libraries (The American Museum of Natural History, for example) have made their catalogs searchable on the Web. And so we have here a paradox, noted by Sullivan: "Users of museum resources can be a much larger, and for some purposes more significant, audience than actual visitors."[17]

A virtual museum means virtual visitors. But we like to keep score, so we count hits at the Web site or searches on the library catalog. Is a virtual visitor as much a visitor as the turnstile pusher? Possibly not, although there is some evidence that the first can become the second, encouraged by advertising, the museum's participation in the community, and the perception that 860 million other people can't be wrong about a leisure-time experience.[18] Fopp sees it this way:

> The museum of the future will probably consist of a real site which
> will be similar in most respects to the traditional museum, and it will

be, as a direct result of hugely increased customer-based [interest]
engendered by the new technologies, vastly more visited by "real" people than ever before.[19]

And so, museums are going extra-mural, in electronic linkages of museums
and museum libraries, and in programming partnerships with other community
agencies, which are often libraries.

Electronic linkages. In Europe, where governments are more directly
involved with museums, there has been a strong impetus toward networks of virtual museums, either as site-links among a number of museums or through the
World Wide Web. For example, a network of twelve museums offers access to
the other eleven from any one of them in multimedia presentations that include
images, text, sound and graphics.[20] Another network, a Web-based effort begun
in 1994, is now divided into pages geographically. The intent is to introduce the
actual museum, as "preparation for a real visit if desired."[21]

Archives are also going virtual. The RAMA Project (Remote Access to
Museum Archives) links various databases and systems in Europe (Janet,
INGRES, ORACLE). And North American archives have evinced interest.[22] The
RAMA Project is one of numerous worldwide efforts to preserve archives and,
simultaneously, enhance their accessibility.[23]

"Without walls" means more than virtuality; it also means "pursuing partnerships that provide gateways to other collections."[24] The libraries in the State
Spanish Museums reflect this concept. Their state-mandated missions make their
collections quite narrow; linked together in a network, their collective databases
cover a wide range of disciplines. This network has enhanced the positions of the
libraries within their own museums from a position of "storehouses for books, of
no importance to a museum" to one of visibility within the national partnership.[25]

Another approach to electronic linkages is found in Oxfordshire, where the
Centre for Oxfordshire Studies "brings together the resources of the museums,
libraries and archives," both physically, in Oxford's central library, and virtually,
through networked access to other sites.[26] "Libraries, archives and museums
need to work together," notes Stephen Price; and much of the effort in Oxford
is programmatic, a path to partnerships being followed by many American museums.

Programming partnerships. While programming partnerships between
museums and libraries are not new, especially in the realm of services to children,[27] they have expanded since 1996, when Congressional fiat expanded the
Institute of Museum Services to include public libraries in the Institute of
Museum and Library Services (IMLS). Under that encouraging umbrella, a number of programs between museums and libraries have been proposed, funded,
and inaugurated.

The American Association of Museums has taken particular note of three such efforts: The collaboration of the Brooklyn Children's Museum, Brooklyn Museum of Art, and Brooklyn Public Library on "Brooklyn Expeditions," an online resource in which the children become active participants; the establishment in Houston of the Library for Early Childhood, a resource for parents and children, housed in the Children's Museum but a branch of the public library; and the Five States American Indian Project, in which the Arizona Department of Library, Archives, and Public Records and the Heard Museum took the lead, working with other agencies and states.[28]

A different approach was taken in Pittsburgh for the 51st Carnegie International (1991-1992). The theme of the exhibition—"issues relating to collecting and display, to the acquisition and circulation of information and hence knowledge"—established an immediate link between and among Pittsburgh's agencies of information and culture. In result, and as a natural collaboration, the Museum of Natural History, the Carnegie Institution's library, the city's public libraries, and the city itself all became both sites for and subjects of the exhibits.[29]

Cheryl Bartholow, reporting on her Brooklyn Expedition experience, notes that the participants "have come to appreciate each other as colleagues and have learned from each other's strengths."[30] And, indeed, herein is the great truth: museums and libraries and the staffs that serve in them do have great strengths, and much to give each other. And it is in working together on a shared vision that the museum's staff and the library staff bring together their information and their knowledge.

The Beckoning Future

When it comes to the form and shape of information, librarians have found that, for many inquirers, the intellectual content is more important than the format or carrier: all manner of carriers—print, electronic, audio—are acceptable to the inquirer as long as the content fills the particular need for information. For example, if the need is to learn the soliloquy, the text of *Hamlet*, a video, or a recording may serve equally well.

But museums are distinctive. Their carriers of content must be *experienced*. Museum objects, along with archives and rare books, still retain a particular resonance, a unique and tangible individuality, and a material presence such that they are in and of themselves a necessary part of the world's intellectual and cultural resources. There is no substitute for feeling the sharp edge of an arrowhead when it comes to understanding flint technology. It is in this way that information becomes knowledge. To go beyond information about flint, to achieve that level of knowledge, one must go where the object is. And, moreover, one must first find out where to go. Electronic resources will provide that answer.

In Summary

We have traveled an information journey beginning with the idea of assuring the centrality of the museum library in the museum information system, then to sharing and exchanging library and collections data within the museum, on to making museum collections data as universally accessible as library bibliographic data, and finally to finding museums and libraries collaborating on projects of benefit to their mutual communities.

All of these things are taking place now, somewhere; there is no reason to suppose they will not continue to do so. The developments we have discussed are a continuum, with the getting-started museum library in a paper environment the most important and significant beginning.

When libraries and museums in the future are linked in a common mission of meeting the needs of the patron and visitor for information, inspiration, and pleasure, all museums should be in a position to participate in the exchange of essential data and information nationally and internationally. To ensure that future participation, it is essential that each museum's library and information services are begun or enhanced now, with assured support and continuing development. Then the museum and the museum library will rightfully lay claim to having been there at the creation—at the opening up of a national and international resource of unimaginable riches.

Notes

1. This is not precisely the connotation of *information* in the Shannon-Weaver communication model, which uses the term in the sense of a transmissible message. See Robert Lossee, *The Science of Information: Measurement and Application* (San Diego: Academic Press, 1990), pp. 3–5.

2. In the strictest sense, information results from thinking about data. As Patrick Wilson postulates in *Second-Hand Knowledge: An Inquiry into Cognitive Authority* (Westport, Conn.: Greenwood, 1983), the only thing found in a document is the text itself; and when we interpret a text—which is to say, think about a text—we discover the information it contains. We have all been guilty at some time or other of parroting data, passing it off as information.

3. Writers in library and information science usually use "information retrieval" when referring to the process of searching a database for names, titles, or bibliographic citations—that is, for data. However, the increasing sophistication of full text databases and the use of artificial intelligence programs (AI) may, indeed, enable us to retrieve information.

4. Forest W. Horton, and Dennis Lewis, *Great Information Disasters: Twelve Prime Examples of How Information Mismanagement Led to Human Misery, Political Misfortune and Business Failure* (London: Aslib, 1991). This is an excellent collection of cautionary tales for the information age.

5. Thomas S. Kuhn, *The Structure of Scientific Revolutions*, 2nd ed. (Chicago: University of Chicago Press, 1970).

6. The systems idea has been around for quite a while. See Duncan F. Cameron, "A Viewpoint: the Museum as Communication System," *Curator* 11/1 (March 1968): 33–40. James Orr describes libraries in the same light in *Libraries As Communication Systems* (Westport, Conn.: Greenwood, 1977.) See also Elizabeth Orna, *Information Policies for Museums* ([London]: Museum Documentation Association, 1987), p. 8. For a prescient discussion of computerizing the museum as an information system, see Mary Van Someren Cok, *All in Order: Information Systems for the Arts, A Report of the National Systems Project, Including the National Standard for Arts Information Exchange* (Washington, D.C.: National Assembly of State Arts Agencies, 1981).

7. Deirdre C. Stam, "Public Access to Museum Information: Pressures and Policies," *Curator* 32/3 (September 1989): 190–198. The issue is not so new after all. See John Cotton Dana, "Libraries and Museums," *Library Journal* 46 (15 June 1921): 539–540. He took note of "the new doctrine that all institutions supported from the public purse, including museums, should show returns for their cost which are definite, and in fair degree measurable."

8. Daniel M. Fox, *Engines of Culture: Philanthropy and Art Museums* (Madison, Wisc.: [Wisconsin] State Historical Society, 1963.)

9. John Cotton Dana, *A Plan for a New Museum: The Kind of Museum It Will Profit a City to Maintain* (Woodstock, Vt.: Elm Tree Press, 1920), p. 41.

10. Ellsworth H. Brown, "Keynote Address," *Museum Curatorship: Rhetoric vs. Reality*, pp. 7–21, Bryant F. Tolles, ed. Proceedings of the Eighth Museum Studies Conference. (Newark, Del.: University of Delaware, 1987), p. 10.

11. Dana, *A Plan for a New Museum*, p. 43.

12. James R. Blackaby, "Integrated Information Systems," pp. 203–229, in: Katherine Jones-Garmil, ed., *The Wired Museum: Emerging Technology and Changing Paradigms* (Washington, D. C.: AAM: 1997), p. 213.

13. Elizabeth Orna, and Charles Pettitt, *Information Management in Museums*, 2nd ed. (Aldershot, Hants (England); Broomfield, Vermont, 1998), p. 9.

14. Ron Chepesiuk, "Organizing the Internet: The 'Core' of the Challenge," *American Libraries* 30/1 (January 1999): 60–63.

15. Katherine Jones-Garmil, ed., *The Wired Museum: Emerging Technology and Changing Paradigms* (Washington, D. C.: AAM, 1997.)

16. For planning guidelines for both types of projects, see Robert L. Anderson, "Creating a Comprehensive Museum-Wide Technology Plan," *Spectra* 24/4 (Summer 1997): 30–32; and Richard Dolen, "The Nature of Museum Data Conversion," *Spectra* 26/1 (Spring 1999): 45–52.

17. Martin Sullivan, "White Gloves and Digital Soup: Museums and the Challenge of Information Technology," pp. 205–215, in: Milton T. Wolf, Pat Ensor, and Mary Augusta Thomas, eds., *Information Imagineering: Meeting at the Interface* (Chicago and London: ALA, 1998), p. 210.

18. Jane Lusaka, and John Strand, "The Boom—and What to Do About It," *Museum News* 77/6 (November/December 1998): 54–60.

19. Michael A. Fopp, "The Implications of Emerging Technologies for Museums and Galleries," *Museum Management and Curatorship* 16/2 (1997): 105–226.

20. Friso E. H. Visser, "The European Museums Network, An Interactive Multi-

media Application for the Museum Visitor," *Information Services and Use* 13/4 (1993): 409–419.

21. Jonathan P. Bowen, "The World Wide Web Virtual Library of Museums," *Information Services and Use* 15/4 (1995): 317–324; and Michelle Koenig, "More Than Museum: WWW of Museums and Other Special Collections," *Information Outlook* 1/12 (December 1997): 15–16, with a listing of museum sites. The Virtual Library is accessible at http://www.icom.org/vlmp, and click on country of interest (accessed August 2000).

22. Guillermo Cisneros, and Ana Luisa Delclaux, "RAMA—Remote Access to Museum Archives," *Information Services and Use* 14/3 (1994): 171–181.

23. Jo Thomas, "The Web Is Easing Access to World's Archives," *New York Times*, (Sunday, 29 November 1998): A1.

24. Milton T. Wolf, and Marjorie E. Bloss, "Without Walls Means Collaboration," *Information Technology and Libraries* 17/4 (December 1998): 212–215.

25. Rosario Lopez de Prado, "Spanish Museum Libraries Network," *Proceedings, Online 96* (New York : 1996), pp. 417–422.

26. Stephen Price, "Whole in One," *Museums Journal* 94 (November 1994): 26.

27. For pioneering efforts, see Hilda L. Jay, and M. Ellen Jay, *Developing Library Museum Partnerships to Serve Young People* (Hamden, Connecticut: Library Professional Publications, 1984).

28. Special issue: "Linking Up Museums and Libraries," *Museum News* 78/2 (March/April 1999): 36–41, 58–62.

29. Amy Jinkner-Lloyd, "Musing on Museology," *Art in America* 80/6 (June 1992): 44–51.

30. "Linking Up Museums," p. 59.

Further Reading

Data and Information

Carbonell, Marilyn. "Some Thoughts on the New Information Culture." *Art Documentation* 10/3 (Fall 1991): 135–136.

Horton, Forest W., and Dennis Lewis. *Great Information Disasters: Twelve Prime Examples of How Information Mismanagement Led to Human Misery, Political Misfortune and Business Failure.* London: Aslib, 1991.

Klapp, Orrin Edgar. *Opening and Closing: Strategies of Information Adaptation in Society.* New York: Cambridge University Press, 1978.

_____. *Overload and Boredom: Essays on the Quality of Life in the Information Society.* New York: Greenwood, 1986.

Kuhn, Thomas S. *The Structure of Scientific Revolutions.* 2nd ed., enl. Chicago: University of Chicago Press, 1970.

Lossee, Robert. *The Science of Information: Measurement and Application.* San Diego: Academic Press, 1990.

Orna, Elizabeth, and Charles Pettitt. *Information Management in Museums.* 2nd ed. Aldershot, Hants (England); Broomfield, Vermont: Gower, 1998.

Wilson, Patrick. *Second-Hand Knowledge: An Inquiry into Cognitive Authority.* Westport, Conn.: Greenwood, 1983.

Museums As Information Systems

Cameron, Duncan F. "A Viewpoint: The Museum As a Communications System and Implications for Museum Education." *Curator* 11/1 (March 1968): 33–40.

Cok, Mary Van Someren, *et al. All in Order: Information Systems for the Arts, Including the National Standard for Arts Information Exchange.* Washington, D.C.: National Assembly of State Arts Agencies (NASAA), 1981.

Orna, Elizabeth. *Information Policies for Museums.* [London]: Museum Documentation Association, 1987.

Orr, James M. *Libraries As Communication Systems.* Contributions in Librarianship and Information Science, no. 17. Westport, Conn.: Greenwood, 1977.

Stam, Deirdre C. "Public Access to Museum Information: Pressures and Policies." *Curator* 32/3 (September 1989): 190–198.

Data Exchange

Jones-Garmil, Katherine, ed. *The Wired Museum: Emerging Technology and Changing Paradigms.* Washington, D. C.: American Association of Museums, 1997.

Wolf, Milton T., Pat Ensor, and Mary Augusta Thomas, eds. *Information Imagineering: Meeting at the Interface.* Chicago and London: ALA, 1998.

Beyond the Walls

Visser, Friso E. H. "The European Museums Network, An Interactive Multimedia Application for the Museum Visitor." *Museum Management and Curatorship* 16/2 (1997): 105–226.

Wolf, Milton, and Marjorie E. Bloss. "Without Walls Means Collaboration." *Information Technology and Libraries* 17/4 (December 1998): 212–215.

Appendix A

Museum, Library, Archives: Official Definitions

Museum: An organized and permanent non-profit institution, essentially educational or aesthetic in purpose, with professional staff, which owns and utilizes tangible objects, cares for them, and exhibits them to the public on some regular schedule.

—American Association of Museums (AAM),
Professional Standards for Accreditation, 1989.

Library: An institution or agency, under the charge of professional staff, which collects, organizes, preserves and makes accessible books, periodicals, audiovisual materials and other information-bearing media for the purposes of instruction, research, reference, or recreation of its clientele.

—American Library Association (ALA),
Handbook of Organizations, 1988.

Archives: (1) The noncurrent records of an organization or institution preserved because of their continuing value; also referred to, in this sense, as archival materials or archival holdings. (2) The agency responsible for selecting, preserving and making available archival materials.

—The Society of American Archivists (SAA),
American Archivist 37/3 (July 1974): 417.

Appendix B

Hypothetical Collection Development Policy

A. Collection Areas

The Hopeful Valley Natural History Museum Library will collect materials in all appropriate formats to support the mission and goals of the Museum. These materials will include, but are not limited to the following:

1. Recognized standard authors and classics in natural history such as Aggassiz, Bartram, Burroughs, Carson, Krutch, Seaton, and Teale, to provide historical perspective;

2. Current field guides, taxonomic keys, and handbooks of the regional flora and fauna, to support field research;

3. Professional and research journals and recent, authoritative monographs in ecology, life sciences, and natural history, to support laboratory research and curatorship;

4. Selected recent, authoritative books and magazines of high interest and general readability level in the same areas of knowledge as section A.3, to support the information needs of museum members;

5. Standard and specialized reference works and indexes, both print and electronic, to support data retrieval and information services and the needs of patrons in sections A.3 and A.4;

6. The most appropriate format for the preservation and presentation of data or information, whether book or nonbook, print or nonprint materials, and including objects, models and regalia, film and recorded sound, and maps, charts, and graphics, to support the various information needs and learning styles of the patrons;

7. The archival records of the Hopeful Valley Natural History Museum and of the environmental education movement in the region, to support the preservation of the history of the Museum and its principal mission.

B. Selection Criteria

1. Selection will be made on the basis of museum staff requests and recommendations for research support; from reviews in standard journals such as *Natural History*, *Journal of Science Education*, *Ecology*, and *Curator*; and on requests from museum members if the title fits the criteria of Section A.

2. Gifts will be subject to the same criteria and will be accepted only under the museum's blanket gift policy.

3. Textbooks will not be acquired unless there is no reasonable alternative or unless they will be direct instructional aids, as in the case of laboratory manuals.

4. Publication date will be within the recent five-year period, unless the work is of a classic nature, as in A.1.

5. Subscriptions will be reviewed annually to assess continuing journal or database relevance, consistent with cost.

6. Duplicate copies of subscriptions to heavily used materials will be given first order consideration so as to make data and information sources as accessible as possible to all the library's patrons.

7. Nonprint media without reviews will be previewed for relevance and accuracy; hardware will not be a consideration in selecting alternative media.

C. Deaccessioning Criteria

1. Weeding will be an on-going process.

2. Old editions of monographs will be deaccessioned when revised editions are received; and superseded materials, or materials which are in error according to current standards in the specific field, will be withdrawn.

3. Circulation *per se* will not be the sole basis for weeding.

D. Serial Publications

1. Binding: The following titles will be bound: *Scientific American*, *Natural History*, *Audubon*, *National Geographic*, *National Wildlife*, *[State] Wildlife*.

2. Journals: Journals (A.3) received in paper form followed by the microfiche volume will be maintained permanently in microfiche and in a one-year paper backfile. Other journals will be maintained in five-year backfile in the Library.

3. Magazines: High-interest magazines (A.4) will be maintained in one-year backfile in the Library; four additional years will be stored in the annex.

E. Collection Development Policy Revision

1. The collection development policy will be reviewed annually before the Corporation Meeting. The following factors will be weighed in making any changes in collection development:

   a. Changes in the Museum: mission, research direction or emphasis, collections and interpretation, educational programs, staffing;

   b. Changes in the Library: expansion or contraction of an information service, type or number of clientele, requests for information service and type of service, processing of materials, data retrieval, and staffing;

   c. Changes in the external environment: the community and its cultural, educational, or economic character; the ecology of the region; regional, state, or national environmental decisions and actions.

2. Before major changes in collection development are undertaken, the collection will be analyzed as to use, currency, supplementation from outside collections, and other bibliometric factors.

3. The Library Staff, the Library Committee of the Board of Governors, and the Education Department will evaluate and approve proposed changes in the collection development policy and will help disseminate the new policies to all board and staff members and other persons and groups as appropriate.

A Step-by-Step Tutorial: Constructing Bibliographic Records According to ISBD/AACR2R Standards

The bibliographic record consists of data taken from the "chief source of information," which in books is the title page. These data may be supplemented, if necessary, by other data derived elsewhere—from the title page verso, for example. The data are arranged in a prescribed order, and set off by specific, nonsemantic punctuation. Using this book as a lab piece, we can construct a 3" × 5" bibliographic record—a description that unambiguously matches the work in hand.

1. Turning to the title page, the chief source of cataloging information, we look for the data to go in the first area of the description—the title and statement of responsibility. The opening element of the title is the *title proper*. If there were a sub title it would be separated from the title proper thus: title proper^:^subtitle. (Spaces in our lab guide will be indicated thus: ^.)

Museum librarianship^

169

Notice that the title is indented a few spaces and that only the first word of the title is capitalized. (We have Melvil Dewey to thank for this bibliographic oddity; he codified the once higher cost of upper case letters.)

2. Next we look next for the *author*. The ISBD convention is to separate the author's name from the title thus: /^. We add the author's name *as it appears on the title page* to the description:

> Museum librarianship^/^Esther Green Bierbaum.^

3. Since there is no further information for the title/statement of responsibility data set, we can use .^ to close it out. Then, to set it off from whatever comes next, we add a defining code, —^, thus:

> Museum librarianship^/^Esther Green Bierbaum.^—^

Note: Had there been other information regarding persons responsible for the book, an illustrator, for example, the data would have been added after the author's name:

> Museum librarianship^/^Esther Green Bierbaum^;^illustrated by Somebody Else.^—^

4. There is a sneaky *edition* notice on the title page, and we have to set it down, surrounded by its punctuation:

> Museum librarianship^/^Esther Green Bierbaum.^—^2nd ed.^—^

5. The last datum from the title page is that of place, publisher and date, which follows what we have already written:

Museum librarianship^/^Esther Green
Bierbaum.^—^2nd ed.^—^Jefferson,
N. C.^:^McFarland,^2000.

The information from the title page is now complete and delineated in such a way that there is no doubt that the bibliographic record refers to this particular book.

6. To clinch the matter, we add the physical description (found by measuring the height and noting the pagination) and the series data, if any:

Museum librarianship^/^Esther Green
Bierbaum.^—^2nd ed.^—^Jefferson,
N. C.^:^McFarland,^2000.
x, 189 pp.^ill.^;^25 cm.

---

7. To create a primary access point (or author entry) we add the author's name, surname first, on the line above the title/statement of responsibility field. In this example, the caret marks we used to emphasize the nonsemantic blanks have been deleted. The finished product looks like this (notes and tracings are also included):

Bierbaum, Esther Green.
    Museum librarianship / Esther Green
Bierbaum.—2nd ed.—Jefferson,
N. C. : McFarland, 2000.
    x, 189 pp. ill. ; 25 cm.

    Includes bibliographical references
and index.

    1. Museum libraries. I. Title.

For more information on creating bibliographic records, consult a cataloging textbook and *AACR2R* itself. The AACR2R is handily arranged so that Part I covers the general rules in Chapter 1, the rules for books in Chapter 2, and the rules for other media and formats in succeeding chapters. Part II provides the rules for access, or entries.

The unique contribution of this cataloging code and its great importance in multimedia collections is the uniform description of all formats and media so that all bibiliographic records pertaining to the library's collection can be displayed in one catalog. Moreover, the areas of the AACR2 description are directly translatable into the fields of the MARC communications format. And, because it accommodates three-dimensional objects and two-dimensional graphics, AACR2R is potentially usable for museum object records as well.

Appendix D

Sources of Catalog Cards and Cataloging Copy

Librarians have two ways to avoid the labor-intensive process of original cataloging exemplified in Appendix C: they can use printed catalog cards, or secure catalog copy. Thus their skills in original cataloging can be devoted to the materials unique to their library and for which neither print nor copy exist.

Though completely original cataloging is relatively rare, the librarian often finds it necessary to edit or correct copy to conform to local standards and practice before the cards are typed. Additionally, the librarian should check all copy and all catalog sets at each step. Typos and other errors can be corrected relatively easily then; later, after filing, they become nearly impossible to discover. One way to improve the accuracy of the catalog is to enlist the aid of patrons in locating and flagging catalog errors.

In a paper-based library, securing catalog cards is a primary concern; hence we outline some of those procedures first.

Sources of Catalog Card Sets

In-house Production by Typing or Copying Cards

There is sometimes no way to get around in-house typing of sets of cards. After the primary access record has been completed, either as original cataloging created from scratch by the librarian or based on a source of cataloging copy (see next section), it is given to a staff or volunteer typist for duplicating. The number of copies made will equal the total number of entries listed in the tracing. Each access point (one per duplicated card) is typed on the line above the primary access point (main entry) and are called added entries, or added access points.

Straight copy typing is one of the library's less joyful tasks. It can wear down the most willing of volunteers. One way to circumvent the drudgery is to use the photocopy machine. The assistant carefully arrays primary access records for copying on pre-perforated card stock. Access points are then typed on the copied cards. This is far from a perfect solution to typing duplicate cards: the photocopy machine must be able to accept the card stock; the cards may blur and smudge; and it is difficult to align perfectly a batch of primary access cards on the photo screen.

A better solution for in-house typing is a memory typewriter, which can spool off the necessary number of cards once the primary access is typed. Headings will then need to be added, of course.

Card Production Software

The next step up from the typewriter is still an in-house means of production, and requires a PC and printer. But for both librarian and volunteer, the software that guides the operator through the input of cataloging data, rearranges and reformats the data, and then prints card sets (all properly headed with traced entries!) can be a both a lifesaver and a dream. Some card production programs are relatively inexpensive, and even with the cost of the sheets of blank cards added in, the price of the software should be amortized rather quickly, relative to the cost of card sets and contingent upon the cataloging load.

The operator simply follows a menu of directions and copies in the data requested from the title page (as we did in our exercise in Appendix C). The program formats the data, adds the punctuation, and instructs the printer to prepare the correct number of access points, complete with the proper headings. To a certain extent the resulting ISBD/AACR2 copy can be tailored to local needs. With some software, it is possible to store the records thus produced on another disk or a tape, eliminating the need to re-enter data when catalog automation is begun. Volunteers are good prospects for data input with these programs.

Printed Catalog Card Sets

From 1901 until March 1, 1997, the Library of Congress set the cataloging standards of American libraries through its Card Distribution Service (now renamed Cataloging Distribution Service.) The Library has listed commercial sources of MARC (i.e., ISBD/AACR2R) catalog cards at //lcweb.loc.gov/cds/csrdsl/html. Some other sources are included in the list that follows. In some cases, the service includes book processing materials (labels, barcodes, and so forth). Some book jobbers also supply card sets and processing with the books ordered. Occasionally, the cards require the addition of call numbers and headings. Some sets marketed as complete still require alterations. Many services create cards according to a local profile, or set of options.

The first of the online bibliographic utilities, OCLC, was originally designed to provide catalog cards for member libraries. It still does so, in addition to creating tapes for automated catalogs and furnishing a wide array of other products and services. Another bibliographic utility, RLG, also supplies card sets. The museum librarian should explore contract options for card production and remain open to future membership in a bibliographic utility network, even though such membership may initially be beyond the means of the small library. If cataloging records for museum objects ever become sufficiently uniform, museums may find using a bibliographic database service for library materials and for object registration a feasible and effective move.

Sources of Cataloging Copy

As a rule, only materials unique to a particular library require completely original cataloging; more often than not, cataloging copy is available from various sources. And while the comfort of copy does not always circumvent the manual labor of producing the set of cards, it does provide guidance, direction, and the form and content of the primary access record.

Cataloging in Publication (CIP)

The bibliographic data found on the verso of the title page of most American publications, called the CIP record, provides very brief cataloging information, and the ISBD punctuation is seldom delineated. The CIP can, however, be a useful source of basic cataloging data, including both Dewey and LC classification and LC subject headings.

Printed Book Lists and Bibliographies

Since the adoption of AACR2 by the Library of Congress in 1980, new records in *The National Union Catalog* (NUC) are in ISBD/AACR2 format, ready to be copied. The *British National Bibliography* (BNB) and *Canadiana* are other national sources of cataloging copy. Other publications, such as

Cumulative Book Index (CBI) and *Books in Print* (BIP), give title page and publication information, but not in standardized form; the records need to be reformatted. Many reviewing sources also give complete enough publication information so that preliminary records can be constructed from them.

Library of Congress MARC Records

These are available on tapes, and on the Internet at http://lcweb.loc.gov/catalog, and FTP. While these latter are formatted as tagged records, the data are complete. (A cautionary note: LCC is supplied as classification, and LCSH for subject access; the records may not conform to the local classification and controlled vocabulary.)

Bibliographic Utilities

Resources such as OCLC (Online Computer Library Center, OCLC), WLN (Western Library Network), and RLIN (Research Libraries Information Network) under certain search-only contracts may be searched for bibliographic records, and this data used to create the main entry record. A terminal and telecommunication with the database are necessary. While the small museum library may not be able to consider the service for itself because of initial costs and continuing fees, it is possible for several institutions to share in cooperative arrangements of various sorts. As already noted, the bibliographic utilities are sources of catalog cards.

CD-ROM Databases

Compact discs are also sources of cataloging copy—and they do not require telecommunication online connections. Obviously, however, a PC with CD-ROM drive is required. The disc databases are based on MARC tapes, and some have older, converted records as well.

NOTE: A cautionary word about any sources of cards and cataloging copy: Before committing the library to any service, the librarian should determine how compatible the records will be with the local catalog. One measure of compatibility is the use of ISBD/AACR2R standards; the best way to determine compatibility is to ask for samples of output. Many services will produce cataloging to the local profile: DDC or LCC classification; LCSH or Sears subject access.

Commercial Suppliers

Suppliers of Catalog Cards

Baker & Taylor
(Includes book processing)
2709 Water Ridge Parkway
Charlotte NC 28217
704/357-3500
Fax: 704/329-8989
E-mail: btinfo@baker-taylor.e-mail.
          com
http://www.baker-taylor.com

Brodart Company
(Includes book processing)
500 Arch Street
Williamsport PA 17705
800/233-8467 x581
E-mail: salesmkt@brodart.com
http://www.brodart.com

Library Associates
FastCat Cataloging Division
8845 West Olympic Blvd.
Ste 201A
Beverly Hills CA 90211
800/987-6794
E-mail: fastcat@primenet.com
http://www.primenet.com/~fastcat

MARCIVE, Inc.
P.O. Box 47508
San Antonio TX 78265-7508
800/531-7678; 210/646-0167
E-mail: info@marcive.com
http://www.marcive.com

OCLC, Inc.
6565 Frantz Road
Dublin OH 43017-0702
800/848-5878
E-mail: marcia_stout@oclc.org
http://www.oclc.org

RLG (Research Libraries Group)
1200 Villa Street
Mountain View CA 94041-1100
800/ 537-7546
E-mail: ric@rlg.org
http://www.rlg.org/ric/ric.html

SANAD Support Technologies
11820 Parklawn Dr.
Suite. 400
Rockville MD 20852
301/231-5999
E-mail: sst@sanad.com
http://www.sanad.com

WLN, Inc. (now OCLC/WLN)
4224 6th Ave. SE, Bldg. 3
Lacey, WA 98503-1040
800/342-5956; 360/923-4029
E-mail: oclc-wln-info@oclc.org
http://www.wln.com

PC-Based Card Production Software

Bibliofile and ITS for Windows

The Library Corporation
Research Park
Inwood WV 25428
800/ 325-7759
E-mail: tloy@tlcdelivers.com
http://www.tlcdelivers.com

Catalog Card Creator ($199)

Right On Programs
778 New York Ave.
Huntington NY 11743
516/424-7777
E-mail: CustomerService@
          rightonprograms.com
http://rightonprograms.com

The Librarian's Helper

(Version 5.0) $150
Scarecrow Press
4720 Boston Way
Lanham MD 20706
800/462-6420
E-mail: tmiller@rowman.com;
          mcralle@scarecrowpress.com
http://www.scarecrowpress.com

Quick Card

The Follett Software Company
1391 Corporate Drive
McHenry IL 60050-7041
E-mail: marketing@fsc.follett.com
http://www.fsc.follett.com

Winnebago PC Cardmaker

Winnebago Software Company
457 East South Street
P.O. Box 430
Caledonia MN 55921
507/724-2301
http://www.winnebago.com

Appendix E

Standard Filing Rules

What follows is a simplification and restatement of the principal rules for filing in dictionary catalogs.* The full text of the rules should be consulted for further examples and finer discriminations; but these six principles will guide nearly all filing decisions in a dictionary catalog.

1. Nothing comes before something.

2. File character by character and word by word:

> New
> New York
> Newark
> News
> Newspapers

3. File **as is** and not **as if**:

> M. Smith
> Miss Smith
> Mr. Smith
> Mrs. Smith
> Ms Smith

Adapted from the American Library Association, Filing Committee, ALA Filing Rules (Chicago: ALA, 1980).

4. File numerals in ascending order of value ahead of alphabetical characters:

> 5 percent solution.
> 1066 and all that.
> About the world.

5. File straight through without regard to punctuation or upper case letters:

> Tennessee history.
> TENNESSEE—HISTORY AND TRAVEL
> Tennessee history renewed.
> Tennessee, John William.

6. File acronyms and initialisms as words:

> A. B. C.
> AASLH
> ABC's

Appendix F

Hypothetical Museum Library Budgets

Conventional Line-Item Budget
(In whole dollars)

	Previous FY	*Current FY*
Books	500	750
Serials	600	850
Audiovisuals	180	200
Supplies	100	100
Computer Fund	800	800
Postage	50	75
Telephone	100	800
Subtotals	2,330	3,575
Salaries:		
Librarian	28,000	30,000
Assistant(½)	11,500	12,000
Subtotals	39,500	42,000
TOTALS	41,830	45,575

Programming Budget
(In whole dollars)

Current FY

	Admin. & P.R.	Educ.	Curat. & Exhbt.	Membs. Servcs.	Lib'y Admin.	Tot.
Materials:						
Books/Serials	20	510	650		20	1,200
Reference Mtrls*	50	450	550	50		1,100
Audiovisuals	50	100		50		200
Supplies:						
General	10	20	20		50	100
Computer	50	100	150	100	400	800
Communication:						
Postage	5	10	10		50	75
Telephone*					100	100
Subtotals	185	1,190	1,380	200	620	3,575
Salaries:						
Librarian	5,000	4,500	3,000	1,500	16,000	30,000
Assistant	1,000	2,000	1,000	2,000	6,000	12,000
Subtotals	6,000	6,500	4,000	3,500	22,000	42,000
GRAND TOTALS	6,185	7,690	5,380	3,700	22,620	45,575

*Online telecommunication charges for information retrieval ($700) are included in the "reference" allocation.

Appendix G

Related Associations and Organizations

Library and Information Science

American Library Association (ALA)
50 East Huron St.
Chicago IL 60611
Tel: (312) 944-6780
http://www.ala.org

American Society for Information
   Science (ASIS)
8720 Georgia Ave.
Suite 501
Silver Spring MD 20910-3602
Tel: (301) 495-0900
E-mail: asis@asis.org
http://www.asis.org

Art Libraries Society of North
   America (ARLIS/NA)
1550 South Coast Highway
Suite 201
Laguna Beach CA 92651
Tel: (800) 892-7547
E-mail: membership@arlisna.org
http://www.arlisna.org

Association of Libraries and
   Information Bureaux (Aslib)
Staple Hall, Stone House Court
London EC3A 7PB
United Kingdom
Tel: +44 (0) 20 7903 0000

Society of American Archivists
   (SAA)
527 S. Wells, 5th Floor
Chicago IL 60607
Tel: (312) 922-0140
http://www.archivists.org

Special Libraries Association
   (SLA), and Museums, Arts and
   Humanities Division (MAHD)
1700 Eighteenth Street, NW
Washington DC 20009
Tel: (202) 234-4700
http://www.sla.org

Museums

American Association for State and
   Local History (AASLH)
530 Church Street, Suite 600
Nashville TN 37219
Tel: (615) 255-2971
E-mail: aaslh@nashville.net
http://aaslh.org

American Association of Museums
   (AAM)
1225 Eye ("I") Street, NW
Washington DC 20005
Tel: (202) 289-1818
http://www.aam-us.org

Museum Reference Center Branch
Smithsonian Institution Libraries
Arts and Industries Bldg,
Room 2235
900 Jefferson Drive, SW
Washington DC 20560-0427
Tel: (202) 357-3101
E-mail: libmail@sil.si.edu
http://www.sil.si.edu/Branches/mrc.
   hp.htm

Index

Terms in the index refer to the museum library *unless otherwise noted.*

AACR2, AACR2 Rev. 41–42; illustrated 43, 44; importance 42; tutorial 169–172

Access points 41, 42–43

Acquisitions 25–27; and museum accessions 19; defined 25; funding 25; order plans 28–29; standards 25; *see also* Ordering materials; and subheading "Ordering," under specific materials, e.g., Books

Administration *see* Management

Air conditioning *see* Climate control

American Association of Museums (AAM) 82, 157

Anglo-American Cataloguing Rules, 2nd ed., Rev. 1988 see AACR2, AACR2 Rev.

Archives 24–25, 123–124; and MARC 124; bibliographic access to 124; conservation and preservation in 124; defined 163; finding aids and indexes 124; in libraries 24–25; in museum collections 27; institutional 25, 123; online 156–157; purpose 5–6; storage 124

ARLIS/NA (Art Libraries Society of North America) 82, 183

Audiovisual equipment 67–68; circulation, 67

Audiovisual materials *see* Nonprint materials

Authority records 49

Automation 134–135; defined 134; history of 135–136; in museums 155; purpose 134–135; uses 138–141

Bibliographic access 40

Bibliographic description 41–42; and AACR2 41; *see also* Bibliographic records

Bibliographic instruction 120–121; clientele 121; defined 120; librarian's role 120

Bibliographic records 41–46; access points in 41, 42–43; creation of 42–44, 139, 169–172; defined 41; filing of 51, 179–180; importance 42, 155; *see also* Cataloging; MARC records

Bibliographic services 97, 106–108; defined 106

Bibliographic utilities: and museums 156–157; as sources of catalog cards

45, 139–140, 175, 177; as sources of cataloging copy 139, 176

Bibliographies 107–108; clientele 108; relation to exhibits 108; skills needed 107–108

Books: as dead weight 61–62, 65; data about 106; ordering 27–30; processing 52–53; selection criteria 25

Budgets: defined 84; hypothetical examples 181–182; line item 84; necessity for 10; programming 85–86

Call number 47, 52–53; as unique identifier 48

Card sorter 130

Catalog cards: commercial sources 45, 139, 174–175, 177; in-house production 132, 140; production from CD-ROM 140; production from computer software 139, 177–178

Catalog records *see* Bibliographic records; MARC records

Cataloging: and museum registration 42; and the Internet 139; as bibliographic access 40; derived, from copy 43–46, 139,

175–176; importance of 40; of various materials 49–50; original 41–43; *see also* Bibliographic records; MARC records
Cataloging textbooks 45
Catalogs 41; as files 41; as furniture 66; dictionary 51; software for 140; union 156; universal access to 156; *see also* OPAC
CD-ROM (Compact Disk, Read-Only Memory): as computer software medium 32–33; as medium for reference works 102, 104; as online database alternative 104, 107, 139; as serials format 26; as source of bibliographic records 48; ordering 32; security for 62; *see also* Computer software
Centre for Oxford Studies 157
CIP (Cataloging in Publication) 41, 44
Circulation 53, 97–100; and confidentiality 53, 98–99; and museum members 99–100; and museum staff 98–99, 100; early automation 135; defined 97–98; equipment for 68; in special libraries 97–98; policies 97; preparing materials for 53; records 97–99; restrictions 54, 100
Classification 46–48; of nonbook materials 47; purpose 46; specialized 47; *see also* Call number; Dewey Decimal Classification (DDC); Library of Congress Classification (LCC)
Climate control 63; and archives 24
Collection development 20–21; initial funding 27; policies 21–22, examples 165–167; reassessing policies 23, 31, 34, 167
Collection management 23–24; defined 19
Collections: archival 24; defined 19; storage 59, 62, 64–65; *see also* Shelving; types of materials in 25–27

COM (Computer Output Micrograph) 135
Computer carrels 66
Computer software 140; in library collections 32; ordering 32–33; preservation 33; security 62
Computer systems 137–138
Computers 133–134; as OPACs 140; functions 133; in libraries 67, 133, 135–138; in museums 133–134, 136; placement in the library 65; security for 62; *see also* Automation
Conservation and preservation 122–123; and electronic media 33, 122–123; defined 24, 122; goals 122; in collection management 24; in initial planning 24; of electronic media 33, 123
Consultants 80–81
Continuing education 82
Copy cataloging 43–45, 175–176
Copyright 118, 126–127 (note 2)
Cross references 49
Curators: and library support 11; services to 98, 108, 117
Current awareness (CA) 116; *see also* Selective Dissemination of Information (SDI)

Data analysis 118–120; and museum administration 120; defined 118–119; presentation 119
Data and information 97, 119–120, 149–152; defined 150, 150–151; exchange within museum 154–155; sources 100–101; quality 150; universal access to 155–156, 159; *see also* Information retrieval
Data conversion 115
Databases: as reference sources 102, 136; bibliographic access to 50; computer software 140–141; costs 103–104; created in-house 136; end-users of 104, 120–121; searching 103, 136; *see also* Online retrieval

Derived cataloging *see* Copy cataloging
Description *see* Bibliographic description
Dewey Decimal Classification (DDC) 46–47
Disaster plans 62–63
Discussion lists 141
Dublin Core (Metadata Core Element Set) 142, 156

End-users 120–121
Entries *see* Bibliographic records
Ephemeral materials 31
Equipment 67–69; traditional 129–132; *see also* Audiovisual equipment

Facilities: criteria 59–60; lighting 63; load-bearing considerations 61–62; location 9; space needs 61–62; space planning 59–61; wiring in 60
Fees and charges 85–86; for online searching 103–104
Filing (of bibliographic records) 51, 179–180
Furniture 63–66; *see also* specific types of furniture, e.g., Seating

Gifts 22–23, 31, 84; of furniture, as memorials 64
Goals: defined 12; influence on library services 13–14; *see also* Museum mission
Government publications 31
Grants 10, 15, 27

Information *see* Data and information
Information audit 109
Information management *see* Management information systems (MIS)
Information politics 21, 155
Information retrieval 102–105, 138–139; alternatives 103–104, 138–139, 143; and Internet 104; and museum staff 104; as data retrieval 150; clientele 104–105; costs 103–104, 105, 138–139; defined 102, 103; evaluation 105; policies 105; vendors for 138

Information services 95–97, 115–124; and museum goals 96; and museum staff 96, 97; as criteria for libraries 20, 109; costs 103–104, 105–106, 117; defined 95; evaluation 83, 105, 126; extended 115–124; kinds 96; planning for 83–84, 109; policies 104–105; psychic costs 87; scope 97; value 109, 115; *see also* Current awareness; Online retrieval; Reference services; Selective dissemination of information

Information systems 152; museums as 152–153

Institute of Museum and Library Services (IMLS) 157

Insurance 62–63

Interlibrary loan (ILL) 99–100

Internet 141–142; and library patrons 104, 120–121, 142; and museums 155–158; and online retrieval 104, 120–121; as cataloging resource 50, 139; as software source 33; cataloging sites on 53; risks 33, 62

Intranets 137–138

ISBD (International Standard Bibliographic Description): and AACR2 41; illustrated 169–172; *see also* AACR2R; Bibliographic records; MARC records

Journals *see* Serials

Labeled records 44 (fig. 3.3), 140

Labels 52–53

Librarians: and access to computers 134; and automation 134–135; and Internet 141–142; and museum administrators 10, 73, 77; and museum public relations 123; and museum staff 21, 87, 116, 117, 118; in partnerships 157–158; museum staff as 11; qualifications 11, 76–77, 90 (note 5); responsibilities 8, 77; *see also* Staff

Libraries: advocacy for 11, 12; and museum administration 11; benefits to museums 7, 153–155; centrality in museums 1, 9, 13, 154; criteria 7–8; defined 163; functions 19–20; funding 10; location 9; negative image 7, 73; organizational placement 73–76; oversight 8; policy manuals 97; purpose 6–7; recognition in museums 155; role in museums 12–14, 154; visitor access to 154; *see also* Special libraries

Library and museum partnerships 4, 154–155, 157–158; value to library 157, 158

Library assistants *see* Staff assistants

Library associations 82, 183; and continuing education 82

Library collections *see* Collections

Library committee 11–12; role 79

Library of Congress: Cataloging Distribution Service (CDS) 45; Catalog cards 45; on Internet 139

Library of Congress Classification 46

Library of Congress Subject Headings (LCSH) 48; sources for 48; *see also* Subject headings

Lighting 59, 63

Local area networks (LANs) 137–138

Magazines *see* Serials

Management: defined 76; hierarchical structure 74; organic structure 75; planning 83–84; staff positions 76–77, 78; structural changes 75

Management information systems (MIS) 119, 138, 140–141; and MARC compatibility 138

MARC (Machine Readable Cataloging) records 42, 135–136, 155–156; AACR2 basis for 42; data included 46–47, 49; defined 42; in

archives 124; in museums 155–156; integrated format (MARC 21) 124, 156; sources 139–140

Marketing 86–88; goals 86; principles 86–87; strategies 87–88

Marking devices, 52–53

Measurement *see* Information services, evaluation; Performance evaluation; Planning evaluation

Metadata 142, 156

Mission *see* Museum mission

Museum administration: and MIS 138; and support of the library 10, 73; services to 97, 102, 105, 107, 108,118

Museum associations 83, 184

Museum educators: and libraries 11, 80

Museum libraries *see* Libraries

Museum members: as library advocates 11–12; services to 98, 99, 100–101, 108, 121; *see also* Library committee; Volunteers

Museum mission: and obligation to objects 153; and patron needs 153, 159; as unifying principle 12–14, 83, 153; defined 12–13

Museum registrars 39; and computers 136

Museum registration 19; and relation to cataloging 39, 40–41, 155; record structure 136

Museums: as information systems 152; defined 163; educational role 158–159; in future 159; in networks 159; purpose 5–6

Newspapers 27

Nonprint materials: circulation 54; in library collections 102; ordering 32–33, 26, 139; preparation 54; storage 50–54; *see also* Audiovisual equipment

Objectives 12–14; characteristics of 12, 83; defined 12; for reference services 105; *see also* Goals

OCLC (Online Computer Library Center) 45, 135, 139, 156, 257, 260; *see also* Bibliographic utilities

One-person library 78; *see also* Librarians

Online retrieval *see* Information retrieval

OPAC (Online public access catalog) 140; screen display 44 (fig. 3.3), 140; searching on 140; software for 140; *see also* Catalogs

Ordering materials 27–33; and automation 28–29; online 39; order file 29; order plans 28–29; receiving orders 29–30; *see also* subheading, Ordering, under specific materials, e.g., Books

Organization *see* Management

Organization of library materials 40–41; defined 40; *see also* Bibliographic records; Cataloging

Outsourcing 40, 139

Ownership stamp 30, 52

Paper, acid-free 122

Partnerships *see* Library and museum partnerships

Performance evaluation 82

Personal computers (PCs) *see* Computers

Personnel *see* Staff

Periodicals *see* Serials

Photocopying: and copyright 118; in catalog card production 174; in preservation 123–124

Photography 130

Planning 83–84, 109, 121, 122–123; and objectives 83–84; evaluation and measurement 84; museum mission as basis for 13–14; preliminary 10; programmatic *vs.* strategic 83–84; value of 84

Preparation of materials *see* Processing

Preservation: defined 24, 122; of electronic media 33, 123; *see also* Conservation and preservation

Processing of materials

52–54; and physical access 40

Procedures manual 52, 55

Professional development 81–82

Programs 108, 121; as service to museum 88, 121; evaluation 84; partnerships 157–158; planning 83–84, 122

Reference and retrieval, difference 102–103

Reference interview 102–103

Reference materials 22, 101–102; criteria 101; databases 103–104; nonprint 102

Reference services 100–101; accuracy 105; by telephone 102, 103, 105; clientele 100–101; costs 101, 104–106; defined 100; evaluation 105; resources for *see* Reference materials

Reports 26, 31

Retrospective conversion 40, 140

RLIN (Research Libraries Information Network) *see* Bibliographic utilities

SDI (Selective Dissemination of Information) 117–118; and confidentiality 118

Sears List of Subject Headings 48; *see also* Subject headings

Seating 65–66

Security of collections 62–63; of archives 124; of archives 124

Selection of materials *see* Collection development

Selective Dissemination of Information (SDI) 117–118; and confidentiality 117, 118; and museum administration 118; and museum staff 117; costs 118; defined 117; profiles 117

Serials: alternative sources 30–31; as CA/SDI resource 116; circulation of 53–54; defined 25–26; in nonprint formats 26; in special libraries 49–50; indexes 106–107; online 26; ordering 30–31; processing 53–54

Service allocation 104

Services *see* Information services; Programs; Reference services

Shelf list 51

Shelving 64–65; capacity 64; compact 64; *see also* Storage

Society of American Archivists (SAA) 82, 124

Space *see* Facilities

Special libraries 8–9; classification in 47; patron instruction in 120; research opportunities 105; serials in 49–50

Special Libraries Association (SLA) 9, 82, 184

Specialized information services *see* CA, SDI

Staff 11–12, 76–82; alternatives 79–80; and confidentiality 117; assistants 78; coherence 79; of museum, as librarian 76, 80; responsibilities 78, 122; security precautions 62; *see also* Volunteers

Standards: role in information exchange 135–136, 155–156

State Spanish Museums 157

Storage: and nonbook media 54; and security 62; planning 60

Subject access 48–49; and classification 48; and vocabulary control 48

Subject headings 48

Tables and desks 65

Technical processes 52–54; defined, 40, 41; *see also* Technical services

Technical services 39–40; and museum registration 39, 41; and reader services 39; costs 39–40; purpose and scope 39–40

Technology 129–144; and preservation 123; defined 129; electric devices 131–132; electronic devices 132–135; in libraries 129; traditional devices 129–131; *see also* Automation; Computers